More than the Truth

Teaching Nonfiction Writing Through Journalism

Edited by
Dennie Palmer Wolf and Julie Craven
with Dana Balick

Heinemann
Portsmouth, NH

Heinemann
A division of Reed Elsevier Inc.
361 Hanover Street
Portsmouth, NH 03801-3912
Offices and agents throughout the world

Editor: Toby Gordon
Production Editor: Renée M. Nicholls
Cover Illustration: Brian Pinkney
Cover Designer: Jenny Jensen Greenleaf
Manufacturing Coordinator: Louise Richardson

The author and publisher wish to thank those who have generously given permission to reprint borrowed material:

Excerpts from the book, NEW KIDS ON THE BLOCK: ORAL HISTORIES OF IMMIGRANT TEENS, By Janet Bode. Copyright 1989 by Janet Bode. Reproduced with permission by the publisher, Franklin Watts, Inc.

Library of Congress Cataloging-in-Publication Data

More than the truth : teaching nonfiction writing through journalism / edited by Dennie Palmer Wolf and Julie Craven with Dana Balick.
p. cm.
Includes bibliographical references.
ISBN 0-435-07216-1
1. Journalism—Study and teaching. 2. Reportage literature—Technique. I. Wolf, Dennie. II. Craven, Julie. III. Balick, Dana.
PN4785.M64 1996
070.4'07—dc20
96-28738
CIP

Printed in the United States of America on acid-free paper
99 98 97 96 EB 1 2 3 4 5 6

Contents

Acknowledgments

This volume is the result of many people joining up and buckling down. We want to begin by thanking the author-teachers who were willing to try a venture that was to be a mix of teaching, researching, writing, and collegial exchange. They signed up without a recipe, came to seminars with strangers, taught in unforeseen ways, and wrote after school and into the nights. Right behind them, we want to thank the students who made these projects possible. They, too, were without a blueprint. And they, too, have given generously of their time, their thoughts, and their writing. Behind the teachers are the colleagues and principals who covered classes, read drafts, and made exceptions. Behind those educators are the urban districts that worked with us to endorse serious school reform: Fort Worth, Texas; Pittsburgh, Pennsylvania; Rochester, New York; San Diego and San Francisco, California; and Wilmington, Delaware. Just in back of the students are families who stayed up to proofread, went to the library one more time, went on field trips, or answered interview questions when they could have gone out, read, napped, or eaten supper.

We also owe thanks to a set of "critical friends"—people who worked along with us, even as they asked hard questions and set unforgivingly high standards: Edmund Gordon, Carol Bonilla-Bowman, Melissa Lemons, Patty Taylor, and Joan Boykoff-Baron. Most recently, we are indebted to the editors and staff of Heinemann, who were willing to work with us even though we were, and remain, a collaborative, with all the varied ideas and voices that implies.

At PACE, this volume would never, ever, have seen the light of day without the tireless energy of Julie Craven and Dana Balick, whose pursuit of detail and timetables made a promise into a contract, and a contract into a manuscript. And also Alex Chisholm, who not only organized us all, but who could not keep from commenting as a fellow writer.

Finally, we want to thank those who, as many as five years ago, were willing to support research on school reform in urban settings. This work grew to become PACE (Performance Assessment Collaboratives for Education), a network of urban school districts committed to high standards of practice for students, teachers, and schools that, historically, have not known sustained support and abundant resources. PACE invented the curriculum seminars that, in turn, gave birth to this series of books. That original generosity—in particular, the willingness to provide a rare five years of work together—has made us remember that the first meaning of the word "foundation" is a solid footing on which a structure can be built. So we thank Alberta Arthurs, Hugh Price, Jamie Jensen, and Marla Ucelli at the Rockefeller Foundation, and Warren Simmons and Lynn White at the Annie E. Casey Foundation.

Foreword: A Word About This Series

Beginning in 1991, with a grant from the Rockefeller Foundation, PACE, an unusual collaborative of urban educators, got under way. In six sites across the country (Fort Worth, Texas; Pittsburgh, Pennsylvania; Rochester, New York; San Diego and San Francisco, California; and Wilmington, Delaware), teams of teachers began creating "portfolio cultures"—classrooms where there was an emphasis on growth towards high common standards and reflection for both students and teachers. The image of a classroom as a culture where a complex network of daily actions supported thinking and imagination provided an important tool for rethinking not just assessment, but curriculum, teaching, and connections to families and the surrounding communities.

It was no accident that this work was centered in middle schools. Early adolescence is one of the most vulnerable—and most promising—moments in the lives of young Americans. Contrary to our stereotypic views of adolescents, many students between the ages of ten and fifteen have their eyes intensely focused on the world "out there." They want to know "What kind of place is there for me—and others like me?" When the answer is harsh and discouraging, we see cynicism, doubt, and disengagement. When the answer is full and reassuring, we see energy, invention, and insight.

Early in our work on creating portfolio cultures, we began to question the usual proposition that as soon as schools are orderly, safe, and respectful, we will be able to launch new kinds of learning. Teachers began to wonder aloud, "Couldn't it be that once learning is under way, we will see orderly, safe, respectful schools?" In the wake of that startling reversal, we began to think about the major learning challenges that young adolescents could take on and enjoy and that could make it possible for many more young people to travel from elementary to high school thinking of themselves as authors, scientists, historians, artists, or mathematicians.

In the process, we developed a unique way of working together that we came to call "Curriculum Seminars." At the heart of each seminar was a major learning task that is possible and important in middle school, but rarely deeply pursued. For instance, we imagined middle schools where students graduated able to

- write powerful nonfiction;
- understand concepts like functions that bridge from the concrete work of arithmetic to the conceptual world of algebra and the representation of complex mathematical and scientific data;
- use the evidence in primary sources to understand lives lived in other times and places.

In order to realize that vision, working groups of teachers became involved in a process to develop curricula that both faced these challenges and made them available to a full range of learners. In the two years that we worked together, teachers, researchers, and outside experts moved through many steps.

- We used portfolios of work from both struggling and accomplished students to investigate what prevents large numbers of students from being successful at meeting these key challenges.
- We took on the role of novice learners in immersions that took us deep into the workrooms and thoughts of adults whose life work depends on the understandings central to journalism, science, and archaeology. This took us out into the city to write journalism; into a collaboration with scientists and mathematicians; to a museum to look at the artifacts of Mayan civilization.
- We designed and drafted curricula to make these big ideas and powerful strategies available to students.
- We taught those curricula and brought the evidence of student work back to the seminar for help, information, and critique.
- We revised and retaught the curricula.
- We thought about the resulting student work in the light of demanding performance standards.

A series of books, of which this is one, is the next-to-final phase of this long-term collaboration. In this step teachers have once again stepped outside their classrooms, this time to become authors. The chapters here are their reflections on what is possible for young adolescent learners—no matter what their history, their income, their country of origin or first language. In this phase, in particular, we began to reflect on a new vision of accomplished and experienced teachers' work. Whatever the specifics, the teachers who were suddenly also researchers and authors insisted that this hybrid work that combined intense classroom engagement with adult reflection was something they never again wanted to be without.

The last step of this work is out of our hands. That is the step where other teachers read and reflect, implement and revise what they find between these covers, and other students engage and invent.

Introduction

On Filing This Book

Dennie Palmer Wolf

Filing—along with physics and painting, chess and forestry—is one of the great acts of human thought. Just take this book. Where does it go? Judging from its cover, it's a book about introducing young adolescents to the demands and rewards of journalism. So maybe it goes on a shelf about literacy, or nonfiction, or maybe it belongs with all those other books about genres. But just inside the front covers, Lee Gutkind, an accomplished journalist and editor, explains how the familiar forms of nonfiction are shifting and changing. Alongside the tried-and-true essay, or feature story, there are new genres of nonfiction, such as "immersion journalism" and "creative nonfiction." In these emerging genres, writers become immersed in a situation or an event that has something vital to teach us about human affairs, such as Christmas tree farming, the changing face of Miami, or the current rage over bagels. But no sooner do they do so than they borrow fiction writers' tools—dialogue, detail, scenes, point of view—to draw us deep into the rows of trees, the smells of a Cuban-Chinese restaurant, or the accent of a man who still thinks in Yiddish. More unnerving still, a teacher-writer-poet, Kellie Brown, follows right after Gutkind. She thinks aloud about her experience of learning to write about immersion journalism and comes up with the conclusion that this brand of observational writing isn't really journalism but is much more like poetry in disguise. So if this book belongs on the literacy shelf, it should sit at the far, slippery, inventive end. After all, if you read it closely, you will end up thinking about how literacy changes, how genres emerge, and how the borders between fact and fiction, prose and poetry are not all that firm.

So if genre turns out to be a shimmering thing, maybe the book belongs in some other, safer, spot. Maybe you would be better off if you slid this book onto your shelf about middle schools—after all, it does portray sixth-, seventh-, and eighth-grade writers taking on the role of journalists. In their chapter, Carol Barry and Kelly Peacock Wright allow us to see how, across an entire semester, students can acquire the many subtle skills involved in creative nonfiction writing: observation, listening, interviewing, and research. They let us see how much young writers are like young scientists learning to assemble the steps of an experiment into a working whole, or archaeologists piecing together the evidence of another civilization.

Then Linda Reilly introduces us to her students, who are newcomers to English. Together they demonstrate how an absorbing investigation can provide the context for building more than a functional second language vocabulary and for pushing to develop a style that is more than just "correct."

In her chapter, Connie Russell-Rodriguez narrates the development of a cross-disciplinary project that used immersion journalism as the setting to bring together American history, civics, and bilingual literacy. Working with photography and video, Kamara Juarez and her sixth graders discovered the power of visual images to fuel research and to raise questions about change in the urban neighborhoods of San Francisco.

But the book will make a rather maverick addition to the middle-school shelf. Yes, the young adolescents in all these chapters chatter, hang out the bus windows, and wander off when they are meant to be sketching or listening to the local historian. But they can also catch dialogue, develop a keen eye for detail, pose challenging interview questions, and get under the skin of accepted truths. The English of their essays is enriched, not hobbled, by other languages and cultures. Their collaborations are full of challenge and urgency. Images and ideas crowd into paragraphs almost too short to hold them. These students are not the usual "bundles of hormones," who are allegedly too erratic for sustained or serious learning. Their bodies may gangle but their brains are just fine. Nor are they self-absorbed individuals too swamped by the throes of identity formation to study someone else's life. As you read these four chapters about teaching immersion journalism, you come face to face with the wrong-headedness of—even the terrible waste caused by—such portraits of early adolescence. At the close, you have to ask if it hasn't been *our* uncertainty about how to combine energy with intellect that has made much middle-school education more placid than challenging, more entertaining than alerting, more self-absorbed than compassionate.

So maybe the book belongs still somewhere else. How about the shelf about American education? You could try to argue that it is about contemporary schooling. But then you would have to find a space for it in between all the volumes that tell of the recent, irreparable failure of American public education, all those narratives of a terrible downward spiral from "the good old days" when students were decent and the halls orderly. But it just won't fit obediently there either. In fact, the book noisily contradicts that overly simplified story. Instead, the work of children and adults featured here reminds us that one of the longest-running promises of America has been public education—what Horace Mann once called "common schools." In particular, the book contradicts the horror stories that have become reflex whenever city schools are mentioned. All of the classrooms described here are in urban areas; they all contain students who are poor, whose first language is not English, or whose families struggle in a nation that refuses to provide a safety net of human services. Still, there are high common expectations. No one coasts. If the students write well, it is because the teachers teach with a fierce determination about quality. Their work, like the work of their students, is both uncommonly strong and commonly achieved. So if the book goes on the American education shelf, it will sit there restlessly.

Actually, if you knew the book's history, you would immediately say, "At least cross-reference it with the other books you own about the professional lives and thoughts of teachers." As described in the foreword, the book is the outgrowth of five years of collaborative work among the faculties of over a dozen urban middle schools. In

1991 they came together as PACE, Performance Assessment Collaboratives for Education, a project that was to look at the feasibility and effects of performance assessment for at-risk students. No sooner did we begin discussing how to assess student work than we realized we could not escape talking about the quality of teaching and learning that underlies any student performance. In the ensuing five years, we have evolved into a project focused on opportunity to learn. Our conversations return again and again to the question of how to make a partnership between quality and equity. Just as often we turn to the question of how teachers might one day have professional lives that honor their work with children, their thoughts, and their insights into public policy.

One of the mechanisms we invented for combining practice and thought was what eventually became known as the "curriculum seminars." These were two-year conversations about teaching and learning in city schools. As a first step, teachers met with experts to master a body of knowledge: journalism, mathematical functions, or archaeology. Then each teacher-researcher designed and piloted curricula to share these ideas with urban students. When the teachers reconvened, they brought samples of the resulting student work. In a seminar focused on that work, teachers acted as critical friends for one another, suggesting how curricula could be made more demanding, more engaging, and more effective with a wider group of students. Based on these exchanges, each teacher revised his or her original work and taught it again, once more collecting student work as proof of what went right and what needed to be thought through again. To forge their experiences in fire, teachers in the curriculum seminars each wrote a chapter about their experiences, acting as both authors and editors of each other's work. The curriculum seminars yielded strong teaching and learning, but they also produced a wholly different kind of conversation from what usually survives in the quick exchanges of hallways or seventeen-minute lunches. All of us had the chance to develop flickers of insight into longer, deeper understandings by adding to, challenging, and refining one another's ideas. Examples of these conversations appear at the end of each chapter as "Reflections from a Colleague."

Speaking to the writing experience, both Kellie Brown in Chapter Two and Julie Craven in her epilogue, "A Teacher's Manifesto," reflect on what is and what ought to be occurring in "professional development" for teachers. Kellie Brown remembers the pleasure of being handed a spiral-bound reporter's notebook and sent out "to find a story" in an unfamiliar city. Using the experience of the curriculum seminars, she sketches what skilled teachers crave if they are to stay on in classrooms, rather than leaving for an assistant principal's office after their third, eighth, or fifteenth year with students. Brown asks for first-hand experience as a learner, not for training sessions or a teacher's edition. Teachers, she points out, want to write their stories themselves, rather than always be written about. They want to be published, just like other thinkers. Too often, she says, good teaching, like good dinner, is totally consumed, leaving no evidence of the hard work that brought it to the table.

Taking up where Brown leaves off, Julie Craven's manifesto calls for collaborative work for teachers. She wants sustained and frank experiences like the seminars, rather than single workshops by outsiders who come and go. She endorses how teachers provided for one another the kind of collegial support to revise and reteach their original curricular designs. She urges a vision of teaching that doesn't force a choice between working in the classroom and making professional contributions to the field of education. But if you slide this book in among other volumes about "teacher training," it could cause trouble. After all, its message is that teachers are closer to poets than puppies.

So, it's true: filing this book is no small challenge. So maybe skip filing altogether. Leave the book lying around, off the shelf, on your table, or poking out of your satchel. Move it around. We think it will stir conversation wherever you slip it in.

1

The Immersion Journalism/Creative Nonfiction Interplay

Living and Writing the Literature of Reality

Lee Gutkind

A Moment of Clarity

It is 3:00 A.M., and I am standing on a stool in the operating room (O.R.) at the University of Pittsburgh Medical Center, in scrubs, mask, cap, and paper booties, peering over the hunched shoulders of four surgeons and a scrub nurse as a dying woman's heart and lungs are being removed from her chest. This is a scene I have observed frequently since starting my work on a book about the world of organ transplantation, but it never fails to amaze and startle me: to look down into a gaping hole in a human being's chest, which has been cracked open and emptied of all of its contents, watching the monitor and listening to the rhythmic sighing sounds of the ventilator, knowing that this woman is on the fragile cusp of life and death and that I am observing what might well be the final moments of her life.

Now the telephone rings; a nurse answers, listens for a moment, and then hangs up. "On the roof," she announces, meaning that the helicopter has set down on the hospital helipad and that a healthy set of organs, a heart and two lungs, *en bloc*, will soon be available to implant into this woman whose immediate fate will be decided within the next few hours.

With a brisk nod, the lead surgeon, Bartley Griffith, a young man who pioneered heart-lung transplantation and who at this point has lost more patients with the procedure than he has saved, looks up, glances around, and finally rests his eyes on me. "Lee," he says, "would you do me a great favor?"

I was surprised. Over the previous three years I had observed Bart Griffith in the operating room a number of times, and although a great deal of conversation takes place between doctors and nurses during the long and intense ten- to fifteen-hour surgical ordeal, he had only infrequently addressed me in such a direct and spontaneous manner.

Our personal distance is a by-product of my own technique as an immersion journalist—my "fly-on-the-wall" or "living room sofa" concept of immersion. Writers should be regular and silent observers, so much so that they are virtually unnoticed. Like walking through your living room dozens of times, but only paying attention to the sofa when you suddenly realize it is missing. Researching a book about transplantation, I had been accorded great access to the O.R., the transplant wards, ethics debates, and the most intimate conversations between patients, family members, and medical staff. I had jetted through the night on organ donor runs. I had witnessed great drama—at a distance.

But on that important early morning, Bartley Griffith took note of my presence and requested that I perform a service for him. He explained that this was going to be a crucial time in the heart-lung procedure, which had been going on for about five hours, but that he felt obligated to make contact with this woman's husband, who had traveled here from Kansas City, Missouri. "I can't take the time to talk to the man myself, but I am wondering if you would brief him as to what has happened so far. Tell him that the organs have arrived, but that even if all goes well, the procedure will take at least another five hours and maybe longer." Griffith didn't need to mention that the most challenging aspect of the surgery—the implantation—was upcoming; the danger to the woman was at a heightened state.

A few minutes later, on my way to the Intensive Care Unit (ICU) waiting area, I stopped in the surgeons' lounge for a quick cup of coffee and a moment to think about how I might approach Dave Fulk, the woman's husband, who was undoubtedly nervous—perhaps even hysterical—waiting for news of his wife. I also felt kind of relieved, truthfully, to be out of the O.R., where the atmosphere is so intense.

Although I had been totally caught up in the drama of organ transplantation during my research, I had recently been losing my passion and curiosity; I was slipping into a life-and-death overload in which all of the sad stories from people all across the world seemed to be congealing into the same muddled dream. From experience, I recognized this feeling—a clear signal that it was time to abandon the research phase of this book and sit down and start to write. Yet, as a writer, I was confronting a serious and frightening problem: Muddled with facts and statistics, tragic and triumphant stories, I felt confused. I knew, basically, what I wanted to say about what I learned, but I didn't know how to structure my message or where to begin.

And so, instead of walking away from this research experience and starting to write my book, I continued to return to the scene of my transplant adventures waiting for lightning to strike. Waiting until the very special way to start my book would make itself known. In retrospect, I believe that Bart Griffith's rare request triggered that magic moment of clarity.

Defining the Discussion

Before I tell you what happened, however, let me explain who I am, what kind of work I do as a journalist/creative nonfiction writer, and how this genre can enrich our approach to teaching literacy—both artistically and academically.

To understand who I am, some definitions are necessary. *Immersion journalists* immerse or involve themselves in the lives of the people about whom they are writing in ways that will provide readers with a rare and special intimacy. For instance, if you read "Action in O.R. #7," the first chapter of my book, *One Children's Place*, you will find me documenting what happens during surgery when a child's life is at stake. These observations grew out of nearly two years of almost living at a children's hospital in order to understand what happens there in the most authentic way possible.

The other phrase that requires definition in this introduction is a broader term, *creative nonfiction*, a concept that offers great flexibility and freedom, while adhering to the basic tenets of nonfiction writing or reporting. In creative nonfiction, writers can be poetic and journalistic simultaneously. Creative nonfiction writers are encouraged to utilize literary techniques in their prose—from scene to dialogue to description to point of view—and be cinematic at the same time. Creative nonfiction writers write about themselves and/or capture real people and real life in ways that can and have changed the world. What is most important and most enjoyable about creative nonfiction is that it not only allows, but encourages the writer to become part of the story or essay being written. The personal involvement creates a special magic that alleviates the suffering and anxiety of the writing experience. Not that writing creative nonfiction is easy. But because writing creative nonfiction is a genuine three-dimensional experience, it provides many outlets for satisfaction and self-discovery.

When I refer to creative nonfiction, I include memoir, or autobiography, and documentary drama, as in the film *Hoop Dreams*, which captures the lives of two inner-city high school basketball players over a six-year period. Much of what is generically referred to as "literary journalism" or, in the past, "new journalism" can be classified as creative nonfiction. This unique combination of literary techniques with immersion as a method for research results in creative nonfiction.

Although many people think of immersion journalism as a new or contemporary genre, it actually has a long history. George Orwell's famous essay "Shooting an Elephant" combines personal experience and high-quality literary techniques. Daniel Defoe's classic of creative nonfiction, *Robinson Crusoe*, is based upon a true story of a physician who was marooned on a desert island. Ernest Hemingway's paean to bullfighting, *Death in the Afternoon*, comes under the creative-nonfiction umbrella, as does Tom Wolfe's *The Right Stuff*, which was made into an award-winning film. Other well-known creative nonfiction writers, who may utilize immersion techniques, include John McPhee (*Coming into the Country*), Tracy Kidder (*House*), Diane Ackerman (*Natural History of the Senses*), and

Pulitzer Prize–winner Annie Dillard (*Pilgrim at Tinker Creek*) to name only a few.

The Five *R*s

Reading, 'Riting, 'Rithmetic—the three Rs—was the way in which basic elementary- and middle-school education was once described. The "Five *R*s" is an easy way to remember the basic tenets of creative nonfiction/immersion journalism: real life, reflection, research, reading, and 'riting.

Real Life

The first *R* has already been explained and discussed: the "immersion" or "*real life*" aspect of the writing experience. As a writing teacher, I design assignments that have a real-life aspect: I force my students out into their communities for an hour, a day, or even a week so that they see and understand that the foundation of good writing emerges from personal experience. This happened to the teachers participating in the PACE curriculum seminars, which triggered adventures in Central Square in Cambridge, leading to a number of interesting new acquaintances, including bookstore clerks, jugglers, fire-eaters, and assorted passersby.

Some writers (and students) may rely on their own personal experience rather than immersing themselves in the experiences of others. For example, in a recent introductory class on immersion journalism, one young man working his way through school as a salesperson wrote about selling shoes, while another student, who served as a volunteer in a hospice, captured a dramatic moment of death, grief, and family relief. Even a novice writer could begin in a police station, bagel shop, golf course, or public service project—all in an attempt to experience, or re-create from personal experience, *real life*.

Reflection and Research

In contrast to the term "reportage," the word "essay" usually connotes a more personal message from writer to reader. "An essay is when I write what *I think* about something," students will often say to me. Which is true, to a certain extent—and also the source of the meaning of the second *R* for *reflection*. A writer's feelings about and responses to a subject are permitted and encouraged in creative nonfiction/immersion journalism, as long as they are written to engage the reader.

As an editor of a journal devoted exclusively to nonfiction prose, *Creative Nonfiction*, I receive approximately 150 unsolicited essays, book excerpts, and profiles a month for possible publication. We only buy one or two. Many are rejected because of an overbearing egocentrism. Writers write too much about themselves without reaching out to readers whose experience may be different. The overall objective of the personal essayist is to make the reader tune in—not out.

Another reason many essays never see the light of print is a lack of attention to *the mission of the genre*, which is to gather and present information, to teach readers about a person, place, or situation by combining the creativity of the artistic experience with the essential aspect of literacy that is the third *R* in the formula: *research*.

Even the most personal of essays are full of substantive detail about a subject that affects or concerns a writer and the people about whom he or she is writing. Read the books and essays of the most renowned nonfiction writers in this century and you find a writer engaged in a quest for information and discovery.

For example, in her first book, *Pilgrim at Tinker Creek*, which won the Pulitzer Prize, and in her other books and essays, Annie Dillard repeatedly offers a wealth of factual information, minutely detailed descriptions of insects, botany and biology, history, and anthropology, blended with her own feelings about life.

One of my favorite Dillard essays, "Schedules," focuses upon the importance of writers working on a regular schedule rather than writing only intermittently. In "Schedules," she discusses, among many other subjects, Hasidism, chess, baseball, warblers, pine trees, june bugs, writers' studios, and potted plants—not to mention her own schedule and writing habits and those of Wallace Stevens and Jack London.

What I am saying is that the genre of creative nonfiction, although anchored in factual information, is open to anyone with a curious mind and a sense of self. The research phase doesn't hinder the creative effort; rather, it anchors invention. Whether it is a book or an essay I am planning, I always begin my quest in the library, for three reasons. First, I need to familiarize myself with the subject. If it is something about which I do not know, I want to make myself knowledgeable enough to ask intelligent questions. If I can't display at least a minimal understanding of the subject, I will lose the confidence and the support of the people who must provide access to the experience.

Secondly, I want to assess my competition. What other essays, books, and articles have been written about this subject? Who are the experts, the pioneers, the most controversial figures? I want to find a new angle, not write a story similar to one that has already been written. And finally, how can I reflect and evaluate a person, subject, or place unless I know all of the contrasting points of view? Reflection may permit a certain amount of speculation, but only when based upon a solid foundation of knowledge.

Reading

In this essay I have named a number of well-respected creative nonfiction writers and discussed their work, which means I have satisfied the fourth *R* in our formula: *reading*. Not only must writers read the research material unearthed in the library, but they also must read the work of the masters of their profession. I have heard some very fine writers claim that they don't read too much anymore—or that they don't read for long periods, especially during the time they are laboring on a lengthy writing project. But almost all writers have read the best writers in their field and are able to converse in great detail about these writers' stylistic approaches and intellectual content. An artist who has never studied Picasso, Van Gogh, Michelangelo, even Warhol, and others is an artist who will quite possibly never succeed.

Most teachers in our PACE seminar agreed that it would be easier for students to accept and satisfy the requirements of the first two "R" words: reflection and real life. Even reluctant immersion journalists will often get quite involved in an experience once they break the ice and commit themselves. But research and, to a lesser extent, reading are more of a struggle for younger students. However, thanks to the information highway, being able to read and research on-line—and not necessarily in the musty stacks of the library—helps make the research phase seem much more like an adventure.

'Riting: The Creative Part of Creative Nonfiction

So far we have discussed the nonfiction aspects of writing about personal experience or immersion journalism. The fifth *R*, the *'riting* part, is the most artistic and romantic aspect of the total experience.

After all the preparatory (nonfiction) work is complete, writers often create in two phases. Usually, there is an inspirational explosion, a time when writers allow instinct and feeling to guide their fingers as they create paragraphs, pages, and even entire chapters of books or complete essays. This is what art of any form is all about: the passion of the moment and the magic of the muse. I am not saying that this always happens; it doesn't. Writing is a difficult labor, in which a regular schedule, a daily grind, is inevitable. But for most writers this first part of the process is rather loose and spontaneous and therefore more "creative" and fun. The second, or "craft," part, which comes into play after your basic essay is written, is equally important—and a hundred times more difficult.

Actually, two parts of this second phase have already been discussed. The first is the research or the teaching element. Enlightening a reader is the unalterable mission of all nonfiction. The second is involving a reader. Just because we think something interesting has happened to us, it won't necessarily stand alone and be fascinating to readers everywhere. To involve a reader a creative nonfiction writer uses several techniques: writing in scenes, selecting details worth telling, and creating an engaging narrative, or frame.

Writing in Scenes Vignettes, episodes, slices of reality, etc., are the building blocks of creative nonfiction—the primary distinguishing factor between traditional reportage/journalism and "literary" and/or creative nonfiction, and between good evocative writing and ordinary prose.

The uninspired writer will *tell* the reader about a subject, place, or personality, but the creative nonfiction writer will *show* that subject, place, or personality in action. Before we discuss the actual content or construction of a scene, let me suggest that you perform what I like to call the "yellow test."

Take a yellow Hi-Liter or Magic Marker and leaf through your favorite magazines, like *Vanity Fair*, *Esquire*, or *The New Yorker*, or return to favorite chapters in previously mentioned books by Dillard, Ackerman, etc. Mark in yellow the scenes, just the scenes, large and small. Then return to the beginning and review your handiwork. Chances are that between 75 and 95 percent of each essay, short story, or novel selected will be yellow. Plays are obviously constructed with scenes, as are films. Most poems are very scenic.

Jeanne Marie Laskas, a columnist for the *Washington Post Magazine*, once told me: "I only have one rule from start to finish. I write in scenes. It doesn't matter to me in which order the scenes are written; I write whichever scene inspires me at any given time, and I worry about the plot or frame or narrative later. The scene—a scene—any scene—is always first."

There's nothing fancy about a scene, by the way. A scene is a story. As a reader, you may not have noticed the proliferation of scenes until now. Good writers understand that craft—the techniques they employ—must remain ever so subtle so that the writing itself never gets in the way of the story they are attempting to tell. Readers should not be aware that they are reading scenes. The idea behind writing in scenes is to make the prose flow so smoothly that readers are entranced, living the experience about which they are reading.

It is equally important to present information scenically and in story form when someone else is talking, as in an interview situation. First and foremost, a scene contains action. Something happens. I jump on my motorcycle and go helter-skelter around the country; suddenly, in the middle of July in Yellowstone National Park I am confronted with twenty inches of snow. Action needn't be wild, sexy, and death-defying, however. There's also action in the "revolutionary bookstore," as in Kellie Brown's essay in this book, or in the classroom. A student asks a question, which requires an answer, which necessitates a *dialogue*, which is a marvelously effective tool to trigger or record action. Dialogue represents people saying things to one another, expressing themselves. It is a valuable scenic building block. Discovering dialogue is one reason to immerse ourselves at a police station, a bagel shop, or a zoo: to discover what people have to say spontaneously—and not in response to a reporter's prepared questions.

Selecting Details Worth Telling Another technique of creative nonfiction may be described as "intimate and specific detail." Through use of such detail, we can hear and see how the people about whom we are writing say what is on their minds; we may note the inflections in their voices, their elaborate hand movements, and any other eccentricities.

"Intimate" is a key distinction when crafting good scenes. Intimate means recording and noting detail that the reader might not know or even imagine without your particular inside insight. Sometimes a detail is so specific and special that it becomes unforgettable in the reader's mind. A very famous intimate detail appears in a classic creative nonfiction article, "Frank Sinatra Has a Cold," written by Gay Talese in 1962 and published in *Esquire*.

In this profile, Talese leads readers on a whirlwind cross-country tour, revealing Sinatra and his entourage interacting with one another and with the rest of the world, and demonstrating how the Sinatra world and the world inhabited by everyone else often collide. These scenes are action-oriented; they contain dialogue and evocative description with great specificity and intimacy. One memorable example is the gray-haired lady spotted in the shadows of the Sinatra entourage: the guardian of Sinatra's collection of toupees. This tiny detail—Sinatra's wig lady—loomed so large in my mind when I first read the essay that even now, almost thirty-five years later, anytime I see Sinatra on TV or spot his photo in a magazine, I find myself unconsciously searching the background for the gray-haired lady with the hatbox.

The Narrative—or Frame The frame represents a way of ordering or controlling a writer's narrative so that the elements of his book, article, or essay are presented in an interesting and orderly fashion with an interlaced integrity from beginning to end.

Some frames are very complicated, as in the movie *Pulp Fiction*, in which Quentin Tarrantino skillfully tangles and manipulates time. But the most basic frame is a simple beginning-to-end chronology. *Hoop Dreams*, for example, the dramatic documentary (which is also classic creative nonfiction), begins with two African-American teenage basketball stars living in a ghetto and sharing a dream of stardom in the National Basketball Association (NBA) and dramatically tracks both of their careers over the next six years.

As demonstrated in *Pulp Fiction*, writers don't always frame in a strictly chronological sequence. My book *One Children's Place* begins in the operating room at a children's hospital. It introduces a surgeon, Mark Rowe; his severely handicapped patient, Danielle; and her mother, Debbie, who has dedicated her every waking moment to Danielle. Two years of her life have been spent within the walls of this building with parents and children from all across the world whose lives are too endangered to leave the hospital.

As Danielle's surgery goes forward, the reader tours the hospital in a very intimate way, observing in the Emergency Room, participating in helicopter rescue missions as part of the emergency trauma team, attending ethics meetings, well-baby clinics, child-abuse examinations—every conceivable activity at a typical high-activity children's hospital. Thus the reader learns from the inside out how such an institution and the people it services and supports function on an hour-by-hour basis. We even learn about Marc Rowe's guilty conscience about how he has slighted his own wife and children over the years so that he can care for other families.

The book ends when Danielle is released from the hospital. I took two years to research and write this book, returning day and night to the hospital in order to understand the hospital and the people who made it special, but the story in which it is framed begins and ends in a few months. Kellie Brown's essay, which came from her winter trip to the revolutionary bookstore, is framed in a similar way.

Back to the Beginning—That Rare and Wonderful Moment of Clarity

Now let's think about this essay you are reading as a piece of creative nonfiction writing, especially in relation to the concept of framing.

This essay begins with a scene. We are in an operating room at the University of Pittsburgh, the world's largest organ-transplant center, in the middle of a rare and delicate surgery that will decide a dying woman's fate. Her heart and both lungs have been emptied out of her chest and she is maintained on a heart-bypass system and breathing on a ventilator. The telephone alerts the surgical team that a fresh and potentially lifesaving set of organs has arrived at the hospital via helicopter. Suddenly the lead surgeon looks up and asks an observer (me) to make contact with the woman's husband. I agree, leave the operating room, and then stop for a coffee in the surgeons' lounge to ponder my own problems, and my fate as a writer.

Then, instead of moving the story forward, fulfilling my promise to Dr. Griffith and resolving my own writing dilemma, I change directions, move backwards (flashback) in time and sequence, and begin to discuss this genre: immersion journalism/creative nonfiction. I provide a mountain of information: definitions, descriptions, examples, explanations. Basically, I am attempting to satisfy the nonfiction part of my responsibility to my readers and my editors while hoping that the suspense created in the first few pages will provide an added inducement for readers to remain focused and interested to the end, where (the reader assumes) the two stories introduced in the first few pages will be completed.

In fact, my meeting with Dave Fulk in the ICU waiting room that dark morning was exactly the experience I had been waiting for. It led to that precious and magic moment of clarity for which I was searching and hoping.

When I arrived, Mr. Fulk was talking with an elderly man and woman from Sacramento, who happened to be the parents of a twenty-one-year-old U.S. Army private named Rebecca Treat who, I soon discovered, was the recipient of the liver from the same donor as Dave's wife's heart and lungs. Rebecca Treat, "life-flighted" to Pittsburgh from California, had been in a coma for ten days by the time she arrived in Pittsburgh; the transplanted liver was her only hope of ever emerging from that coma and seeing the light of day.

In the next half-hour of conversation, I learned that Winkle Fulk had been slowly dying for four years. She had been bed-bound for three of those years, as Dave and their children watched her life dwindle away, as fluid filled her lungs and began to destroy her heart. Rebecca's fate had been much more sudden; she had contracted hepatitis in the Army—and crashed almost immediately. To make matters worse, Rebecca's new husband, faced with the specter of a dying wife, left her.

Later I discovered that the kidneys from this same donor had also been brought back to Pittsburgh and would be implanted the following day into two young people, ages twenty-one and twelve, from Middle Eastern countries. The corneas from this donor would be transplanted into two African-American women.

As I sat in the darkened waiting area with Dave Fulk and Rebecca's parents, I suddenly realized what it was I was looking for, what my frame or narrative element could be. I wanted to tell about the organ transplant experience, and what organ transplantation can mean from both a universal perspective—medically, scientifically, internationally, interracially—and a personal one, for patients, families, and surgeons. Rebecca's parents and the Fulk family, once strangers, would now be permanently and intimately connected by still another stranger: the donor, the person who inadvertently gave his life to provide hope and perhaps salvation to two dying people. In fact, my last quest in the research phase of the transplant book was to discover the identity of this mysterious donor and literally connect the principal characters. In so doing, the frame or narrative drive of story emerged.

Many Sleepless Nights begins when fifteen-year-old Richie Becker, a healthy and handsome teenager from Charlotte, North

Carolina, discovers that his father is going to sell his sports car, which Richie hoped would one day be his. In a spontaneous and thoughtless gesture of defiance, Richie, who had never been behind the wheel, secretly takes his father's sports car on a joy ride. Three blocks from his home, he wraps the car around a tree and is subsequently declared brain-dead at the local hospital. Devastated by the experience, but hoping for some positive outcome from such a senseless tragedy, Richie's father, Dick, donates his son's organs for transplantation.

Then the story flashes back a half century, detailing surgeons' first attempts at transplantation and all of the experimentation and controversy leading up to the development and acceptance of transplant techniques. I introduce Winkle Fulk, a mother of four dying with an incurable heart disease, and Rebecca Treat, a recent high school graduate with hepatitis, who is in a coma and near death.

Richie Becker's liver is transplanted into Rebecca Treat, while his heart and lungs are sewn into Mrs. Fulk by Dr. Bartley Griffith. The last scene of the book 370 pages later is dramatic and telling; it finishes the frame three years later when Winkle Fulk travels to Charlotte, North Carolina, for a reunion I arranged, to personally thank Richie's father for his son's gift of life.

> At the end of the evening, just as we were about to say goodbye and return to the motel, Dick Becker stood up in the center of the living room of his house, paused, and then walked slowly and hesitantly over toward Winkle Fulk, who had once stood alone at the precipice of death. He eased himself down on his knees, took Winkle Fulk by the shoulder and simultaneously drew her closer, as he leaned forward and placed his ear gently but firmly between her breasts and then at her back.
>
> Everyone in that room was suddenly and silently breathless, watching as Dick Becker listened for the last time to the absolutely astounding miracle of organ transplantation: the heart and the lungs of his dead son Richie, beating faithfully and unceasingly inside this stranger's warm and loving chest.

References

Ackerman, Diane. 1990. *Natural History of the Senses.* New York: Random House.

Defoe, Daniel. 1992. *Robinson Crusoe.* New York: Knopf.

Dillard, Annie. 1988. *Pilgrim at Tinker Creek.* New York: HarperCollins.

Gutkind, Lee. 1990. *Many Sleepless Nights.* Pittsburgh, PA: University of Pittsburgh Press.

———. 1991. *One Children's Place.* New York: NAL-Dulton.

Hemingway, Ernest. 1978. *Death in the Afternoon.* New York: Macmillan.

Kidder, Tracy. 1985. *House.* Boston: Houghton Mifflin.

McPhee, John. 1977. *Coming into the Country.* New York: Farrar, Straus and Giroux, Inc.

Orwell, George. 1950. "Shooting an Elephant." San Diego: Harcourt Brace and Company.

Wolfe, Tom. 1984. *The Right Stuff.* New York: Bantam Books.

2

When a Poet-Teacher Gets to Be a Writer

Kellie Brown

In my life as a teacher, I have sat in any number of writing workshops listening to what I *could* do with my students next time I teach fiction or poetry or research. Sometimes, when I've been lucky, the workshop leader asked us to write. For five or ten minutes we were to open our notebooks, take out a pen, and taste what we would do if *we* were actually writing. In the quiet that followed, the prospect of being authors—with time, ideas, other writer colleagues, a tough-minded editor, and a publisher ready to give us a glossy cover—danced out there like a fat letter addressed to someone else.

But not so with our seminar on immersion journalism. Before I left Fort Worth for a weekend seminar at PACE, in Cambridge, a packet of writing arrived in my school mailbox. My preseminar assignment was to get to know these authors as my colleagues: What were they up to? How did they make their pieces work? Not because someday I was going to write the six rules of immersion journalism up on the board for my sixth graders, but because the seminar we were about to begin was founded on the notion that I, Kellie, would become a journalist, at least for a while.

From the very first hour of the seminar's first day, when we crowded around the table looking sideways at one another, we were writers—without question, but within limits. We met one another, and also Lee Gutkind, the journalist who was going to be our guide, teacher, reader, and eventually our editor. Right away Lee asked us what made the articles we had received on Tom

Cruise and bush taxis different from "pure" literature, what set them apart from "straight" journalism. Since he was sure we knew, we spoke up like experts: the curiosity about reality, the research tucked into the interviews that worked like I-beams in the building of the story, the detail, the dialogue, the movie-like feeling of being caught up in a scene . . . What was our reward? Not being allowed to settle into the soft comfort of talking about other people's work. Lee produced a stack of reporter's notebooks: the spiral-bound skinny ones that every "real" reporter flips open at the first flush of a story. "Go out and find a story," we were instructed. We got subway tokens and walking directions to the artsy-hip-bohemian heart of Cambridge's Central Square. It was our "job" to find a person, a place, an event to write about with all the instinct, integrity, and language tools we had identified only moments before. The context for our search was a quote from Barbara Jordan: All the people want is an America as good as its promise.

When we paused and tried to push questions between us and the work ahead, Lee only offered, "Look around you. Listen. Find out just what that promise might be, and if it's being kept."

I found my story in what someone called the "revolutionary bookstore." It was just inside the Square. I considered going further down the street and hunting up other options, but I could sense the danger: it would net me no story and all the "should'ves" and "might'ves" I could stomach. So I went with the revolution. A few hours later, I left the store with a three-dollar signed copy of a book by Walter Dean Myers (of *Fast Sam, Cool Clyde and Stuff* fame) and more importantly, my observations—the makings of a story of my own.

Later that same day, back in our writing "classroom," Lee insisted, "Trust your memory while the experience is fresh—but *only* when the experience is fresh." We wrote furiously, going after every detail, rushing to create notes. We bent over our spiral notebooks, sorting out the story from the chaff (or at least trying to seem as if we had not just strolled about on that warm winter day). Lee insisted that we read aloud, with no apologies: "not finished" was no excuse. People I had met hours before as classroom teachers had found America's promises in a coffeehouse and beside the clothing racks at Woolworth's:

> Start with that strange little notch in the middle of her forehead, between her brushed-up eyebrows. The place went dim except for the smell of coffee in the air and the rapid prancing of servers behind the counter. What I vividly remember were her eyes; the way the soft, silver-blue iris had distinctive darker outlines and nearly imperceptible wrinkles at their corners. "What if wrinkles could tell stories?" I asked myself.
>
> *Clyde Yoshida*

> A quick visual survey of the aisles of Woolworth's produces a UN tally of folks from all over the globe. Chinese, Ukrainian, Jamaican, Hispanic. Why are they here *now*, lunchtime on an exceptionally warm December day? Is it some element of American culture which attracts them? The orderly rows of mundane household items? Or is it the comfort of cleanly swept wooden floors and kindly grandmother-types to wait on you? Can they understand America better by coming here?
>
> *Linda Reilly*

I was a writer among writers.

Still later that night, up in our hotel rooms, each of us continued to write and write. The next morning, together again in our seminar, we read again and talked: "Oh, I hadn't thought of that angle." "That's a good way to say that." "When did you start/stop/give up?" When it came to my turn, I read out what I had so far:

> "That's the Revolutionary Bookstore." It was pointed out to me across a wide, busy intersection in Central Square. In the window were familiar and unfamiliar titles, and inside, not a soul. As I looked around the inside, I figured some intense young radical/bohemian was in the back, counting books or printing fliers. But what I saw when I came around an island bookshelf in the center of the store was an adolescent-looking white guy asleep with his feet on the desk. He woke up when

the phone rang and he groggily began giving directions to the store to the woman on the phone. He came over to where I was standing and asked me what the name of the street was out front. "I'm from Texas, I'm no help," I apologized. He mumbled something about not being able to help anyone who was from Texas and went back to the phone. After he hung up, he asked me what I was doing in Cambridge. I explained that I was here as part of a study on ways to better teach kids, urban kids. Still a little groggy, he emphatically offered the opinion that "we should take the money from suburban white kids and give it to the urban kids, that's what we should do." I observed that his socially irascible comment only highlighted the fact that even he viewed urban/suburban issues in nonwhite/white terms.

His name was Joel, I found out much later. When I first saw him in the store, he looked like a teen-aged loner. Up close, he looked like a middle-aged loner with an island of thin blond hair in the middle of a rapidly receding hairline. He wore wire-rimmed glasses and a defensive, peeved look that could have come from a lack of sleep or his status as a full-time idealist. He told me that he had dropped out of high school, gotten his GED, and through a series of decisions and nondecisions, "ended up here." He was twenty-one. He used words like "boring," "irrelevant," and "fed up" to describe his school experience back in Detroit. He liked learning though. He loved history, and the grogginess receded as he began describing how he had been studying on his own and was fascinated with discovering the causes for why things are they way they are today—that there was a world before 1940. As I listened to him talk I thought about Barbara Jordan's patient explanation that what she wanted was "an America as good as its promise." I looked at the titles for a while: *For the People, Pedagogy of the Oppressed, Stolen Legacy, The Boiled Frog Syndrome*. Joel seemed to agree with her on at least one or two of the points of the promise, as did the entire store.

Joel didn't learn how to learn until he started learning on

his own. That wasn't something they taught you in school, he pointed out to me. And when his little brother Jacob faced frustration in school, he says he told him that even if he got nothing out of it, learn how to learn. But he didn't expect him to drop out; he had athletics to keep him there.

A tall, black man with a Hispanic accent came in and asked about a poster for $11.95. I returned to the titles, but my attention was on the conversation. "Do you have anything smaller, just this?" he asks, gesturing toward the framed face of Martin Luther King, Jr., in the picture. Joel doesn't know, so they go to the poster bin to look. I notice a selection of Spanish-language literature and ask if there is a large Spanish-speaking community here. "Oh *yeah,*" replies Joel. The tall man laughs that short burst of laughter that usually means "you'd better believe it." But I cannot draw him into a conversation about Spanish speaking in the classroom. He simply tells Joel he will come look again later and leaves, tall and big and silent on the issues of speaking Spanish in a stubbornly English land.

Almost immediately another man comes in asking for a handbook of basic phrases and street signs for a non-English-speaking person. No, Joel replies, and tries to think of where he could find such a practical thing.

The solution is lost in the ringing of the phone and the entry of another customer. "No, we're strictly a volunteer-run operation that depends on donations. We can't buy books. Uh-huh. Well, you're welcome to bring them down anytime. Okay ma'am, good-bye." He hangs up the phone. From the back of a tall bookshelf comes the oddly southern voice of a woman asking loudly, "Do you buy used books?"

I'm looking at the titles again: *Ain't I a Woman?, Malcolm X, Since Silent Spring, Interrace: A Magazine for Interracial Couples, Families, and People, Blaming the Victim,* T-shirts exhorting us to save the Earth and share it, *How People Get Power, Everyone Wins!*

The store seems to be a type of response to the exclusionary, zero-sum nature of the mainstream. People with small voices, strange voices, loud, discomforting, or unpalatable voices are given a place to speak here. Lucy Parsons herself, the store's namesake, was just such a voice. She was a black woman who lived in the 1800s and married a white man in Waco, Texas. Needing to save her life for that choice, she and her husband moved to the East where she worked for years in the labor movement. As the need existed then, so the need exists now for welcoming places for the pieces that don't fit so easily into the prescribed lines of the American Dream.

Joel leaves momentarily to flag down the woman to whom he had given directions earlier. He returns with a dark brown shopping bag and resumes his place behind the desk. He becomes animated as he shows me his great find—fifty or more maps and an atlas for thirty dollars. He collects maps, some to display, but most to use as references for his studies in history. I look closely at one and we talk of *National Geographic* like coffee magnates speaking of Brazil.

Joel is flying in the face of all the efforts to conform him, to rub him smooth and malleable, and he's learning. Whatever else Joel does or doesn't do, believes or doesn't believe, there is this: he is excited about and engaged in maps and history. He volunteers three days a week at the revolutionary bookstore, and holds down a paying job that wears him out from the looks of it. This exhausted, old-looking twenty-one-year-old puts his money where his mind is—thirty dollars just today. A room full of books on the promise and its keeping being sold by a man who is not waiting for his part of the promise to be kept.

Lee spoke up about what he saw coming in the piece. A surge of questions followed. I was exhilarated. I admit I had visions of glory: I was going to write my piece over. I was going to make it work. I was going to write the Great American Piece of Immersion Journalism. Then I went home. My deadlines and commitments met me at the door of the plane. Today became tomorrow, tomorrow became sometime, and sometime is still waiting.

Neither *Rolling Stone* nor *Texas Monthly* has published my piece on the revolutionary bookstore. But other quite unpredictable, very "writerly" things have happened. We each left the first round of the seminar with an assignment. We would finish our own pieces and then, with the experience still alive, we would figure out how to engage our students in the kind of alert, precise writing in which we had apprenticed. In February, we would meet in Fort Worth for a "winter summit." There we would share our teaching plans, just as we had shared our journalism—each of us an author, each of us a tough critic. We would work on a journalism project with our students in the spring, collecting their work, and our own reflections. In July, we would reconvene in Cambridge to share what we had learned about teaching immersion journalism in our very different classrooms. After that, we would write a book (this book) together about our experiences as writers and teachers of immersion journalism. In short, our pact was nothing less than the pledge that, less than two years after we first wandered through Central Square, armed with our notebooks and Barbara Jordan's words, we would be authors on our way to publication.

I left with my marching orders, the same as everybody else's. But gradually my assignment took on a shape of its own. Sometime in the months after the first meeting of the immersion journalism seminar, I was brave (crazy?) enough to send several of my poems to other people in the seminar. They wrote back to me, not as their buddy Kellie, or as another teacher of middle-school English, but as a writer, a poet. Through letters and e-mail, we went over my work: the words, the line breaks, the final lines.

As the deadline for the manuscript chapters came closer, I got the assignment to write the chapter about the seminar itself. I was to use my piece about the revolutionary bookstore. Now back in the daily routine of William James Middle School, and being Ms. Brown, I wrote the piece I thought I should. It was—at least in its first draft—about why we should bother to teach this kind of journalism to middle-school students. It was well written and to the point. I dusted off my hands and considered myself free from nagging deadlines. But then the draft came back (they have a way of doing this). There was a note toward the end:

> Kellie—I am wondering something. Several months ago you shared two drafts of several poems you were in the process of writing. Each was full of closely observed detail. While I was working on this editing, I kept thinking, "Now isn't there some way to pull in those poems?" I have no idea how you feel about making them public. But they kept jumping to mind . . .

Unsure where the revolutionary bookstore and the poems would meet, I sent off two poems: one about picking greens with my mother, and this one about two peppermints. They both really happened; they each had one foot in reality, one foot in literature. Perhaps that was the link to immersion journalism:

Snow and Peppermint
My mother drove me miles and miles
for Santa and a tree.
The man said Santa was out,
but he offered me a peppermint.

Over a few snowy hills we searched
For a tree and I felt the peppermint
in my pocket, thinking how I would enjoy it
Because it was Christmas.

I asked for one for my sister
and he laughed
But I really wanted to give her one
because it was Christmas
and I was feeling magnanimous
and I thought she would enjoy it.

My mother found a tree she liked
So we took the tree and the peppermint and
the man who wasn't Santa
back to the car.

He loaded up the tree for us and
Santa came as we were leaving
He gave me another peppermint.

In the car, I stared out the window
and watched the miles and the snow
and I ate both peppermints
on the way home.

For the next several drafts, the poem hung sort of suspended and out of place in the draft. Letters and drafts shuttled between Cambridge and Fort Worth as we groped and juggled our way toward understanding whether it belonged and why. At one moment, we thought the point had something to do with the necessity for closely observed detail that cropped up both in the journalism and the poems. We were headed, I think, toward the argument that what students learned in journalism could be transported to other kinds of writing. So the note on that draft asked me to think aloud on paper about the parallels between those two pieces of writing. Partly stumped, partly exasperated, here is all I could write back:

> I have tried to come up with intelligent discourse on the tools I used to write this, but I am woefully ignorant on that topic. And I can't fake it. Do you know how I wrote this? For the last several years I have returned again and again to this scene in my mind and rewritten it and reworked it until what was on the paper looked like what was in my head. I don't know that I could articulate in a practical way what that took. When I write, I rely on both the subtle differences in words and the rhythms that I learned listening to Dr. Seuss (I swear) and Sunday preachers . . .

Again, it was enough. But my draft came winging back (again). In pencil, cramped into the margin, was this note, in handwriting I didn't recognize:

> My reaction, if you want one: It's not mechanics, that's just the point. Dr. Seuss and the preacher are the point.
> Listening + Thinking = Writing
> (I just made that up.)

This wasn't from the editors. It came from someone who, by day, works in the offices at PACE, but who, by soul and by trade, is a writer. Everyone had a finger in this chapter, everyone had an opinion, everyone was rooting for it.

It came home to me: I remembered those occasional ten minutes in workshops when we, as teachers, had been asked to write. That was the point. The seminar had been about me as a writer first, and only then as a teacher of writing. There are days when I drive to or from school fighting with the last line in that poem about picking greens. In that time, I am murmuring it in my mind and listening to Dr. Seuss and the preachers with my ears. Along its funny unpredictable path of drafts and notes, my work in immersion journalism ended up saying: "What a waste it is to leave that conversation in the parking lot with the last pull of the parking brake. Teach from it."

What exactly do I mean? It goes like this: My short and happy life as an immersion journalist turned on a light in the secret room where I've been keeping my poems. I began to think about teaching writing *as a writer*. For instance, the noise and hubbub around my work was vital. In the very first days of the seminar in Cambridge, I was a writer among writers. I wanted to improve my piece because I had the permission to take my choices seriously and I was among peers who were taking theirs every bit as seriously. I went away to write the greatest piece of American journalism ever, but, instead, I sent back two poems. No matter. Questions, pokes, prods all came flying back. Who says writing is a solitary act? (Maybe first drafts are—I recall that first night alone in my hotel room.) But the talk around the table the next morning was as public and social as it gets. Professional writers, amateur writers, sometimey writers (like teachers who want to climb inside what it takes instead of just announcing what's involved) all need discussions with others. Where else are you going to get those long-time "others" inside your head—those voices that say, "Yes, that's good, hold on to that part" or "Guess this one isn't finished yet"? My students are no different than I am. They need those same external efforts turned into internalized instincts. (Just as a teacher develops a sixth sense for what teaching takes—an intuition that you do not have in your first year.) And they need what goes along with those voices: a thick skin, flexibility, and the ability to sift through all that gets said to recognize what is valid and what is useless.

I also began to think about time—the real time it takes to write. Even where we faithfully practice "the writing process," too often all the incubation and revision students do occurs sharply within the three days or the several weeks that the particular assignment or project lasts. But with my own piece on the revolutionary bookstore, a first draft got written inside the several days of our seminar. The final draft, however, is still unfinished. This piece about the seminar is now in its third draft, spaced out across half a year. All this has made me think that much of the writing we do in schools is really stranded somewhere between the tempo of daily assignments and genuine writing time. What if we let students keep pieces alive throughout a year? Even across years?

And what is this writing process we all have been taught and that we pass along to our students like keys to the kingdom? Brainstorming, drafting, peer editing, revision, publishing: okay for the *how*, but where is the *what*? Lee never once pretended that those generic steps would find us our story. Instead, he shared "insider" tools: visiting a place over and over until you found a story; being willing to follow out unexpected lines of conversation; waiting to take notes until after you left the scene, when the important details hung in memory. I was delighted to learn those trade secrets. The note in the margin of my draft tells me I owe my students the same. Not broad talk about "rhythms" or "details," but the truth about Dr. Seuss and the preachers. They deserve the voices of writers, not just talk about writing.

I realize I haven't given you a step-by-step rule book or recipe for teaching immersion journalism. It's more about *learning* immersion journalism. It is a vote for teachers as authors. For teachers to be let loose in Central Square, to be given the question hidden in Barbara Jordan's quote, to read aloud, to be asked to include, not forget, their poems, and to hear that Dr. Seuss and Sundays spent listening in church are just the point.

The work of teaching is hard. Particularly if you choose to teach students who need it most. Especially if you elect to stay in it for the long haul. "Professional development" in the form of workshops *about* writing are not enough. No one who drives to school wrestling with the last line of a poem about greens picking can survive on ten-minute simulations of being an author. We need more. It has to go as deep as being expected to produce a piece. It has to last not an afternoon or a Saturday, but months. It has to be the sort of busy body village work where all kinds of people stick their nose into your business. It ought to end up with being published.

References

Myers, Walter Dean. 1988. *Fast Sam, Cool Clyde and Stuff*. New York: Puffin Books.

Reflections from Colleagues

Lee Gutkind and Dennie Palmer Wolf

Throughout Kellie Brown's piece on the revolutionary bookstore you can almost sense her eye traveling up, down, and around, seeking just those few details that will send a picture of the place, the clerk who doesn't know the name of the street in front of his store, his peeved look coming from his status as a "full-time idealist." Reading it, those of us who knew that Kellie wrote poems asked her about the connection between the two sets of images. The result? The peppermint poem found its way into her essay with all its careful choices: "My mother drove me miles and miles/for Santa and a tree"; "I . . . watched the miles and the snow . . ."

Reading the revolutionary bookstore piece, the essay, and the poem side by side, Lee Gutkind wrote this to Kellie:

> Dear Kellie,
>
> I am very impressed with your prose—the way you put words together and the pure passion behind those words—and with how you have structured your essay. I like how you begin your narrative with a story, and then when your reader is squarely hooked, you go off on interesting and related tangents before bringing the story to a close. In this way, you put the classic frame or story structure to good use. The detail you select to capture the bookstore—especially your succinct but evocative characterization of Joel—is admirable. I especially like your use of the Barbara Jordan

> quotation ("All the people want is an America as good as its promise.") and the way you keep coming back to it like a refrain. In that way it becomes almost a metaphor for what you and other teachers are doing in the classroom. You have certainly found a focus and a message that holds my attention.
>
> But midway through the essay, I find myself losing hold of that focus. That happens just about the time we leave the bookstore. In another draft, I wonder if you could be more specific about the connection between your immersion journalism experience in Cambridge and your own poetry. On the surface, journalists and poets seem miles apart in temperament and objective, but in actuality they are both in search of a truth that is often established through the use of specific detail. The closeness of poetry and journalism can be illustrated in countless ways. Diane Ackerman (*Natural History of the Senses*) published a half dozen books of poetry before beginning to write her lush and evocative nonfiction; no prose is more poetic than that which appears in Annie Dillard's Pulitzer Prize–winning nonfiction book *Pilgrim at Tinker Creek*.
>
> It leaves me wondering—in fact, wanting to know—what you will make of this connection in your own writing and teaching.

Reading Kellie, and then seeing Lee's response, made Dennie think about how we teach writing: Ask any eighth grader what makes for good writing and he or she will, without dropping a stitch, reply, "Details, you have to have lots of details." How do they know that? Along the margins of their pieces we have written "Details!" "Show me," and "Not the same old words" hundreds, maybe thousands of times. And in their short careers they have probably done at least that many lessons adding adjectives or sliding adverbs into sentences. Most scoring rubrics at least imply that part of what separates poor from ordinary from remarkable writing is—detail.

No one in his or her right mind wants students writing the spare prose of textbooks or the stubby sentences of basal readers. But have we really been telling the truth? Take these two sentences:

> The old man with the shaggy gray eyebrows leaned his bony elbows on the dark oak table.
>
> The old man leaned into the table.

The first one certainly has a high detail population, but the second may offer a reader much more about the bone-tiredness of old age. If so, it comes from choosing just two words carefully: "leaned" and "into." Or take a newspaper article about Ron DeCarava, who, beginning forty years ago, began to create the photographic record of jazz. The book is called *The Sound I Saw*. Look at the power of that little jump from the expected "heard" to the startling "saw." Later in the article, DeCarava explains that both jazz and photography are improvisations that depend on a respect for the flow of time; "in between that $^1/_{15}$ of a second, there is a thickness." All he said was "thickness." A single noun, taken on a slant.

So we are fooling ourselves and our students when we write "Details!!" in the margin. We don't really mean a frosting of how big, how frightening, how blue, how lovely. We want immediacy, not stuff. That should change how we teach journalism, or any other genre for that matter. We can almost imagine writing "Subtract!!" in the margin. Or asking students to take a short story and cross out and cross out, until they have those few phrases or images that "say it all." We can imagine turning back a piece of writing and saying that we want it to jump to life—but all that can be changed are the verbs—or maybe the prepositions. We would be after a certain "thickness"—gotten through a deliberate thinness.

The air is full of calls for school reform. And thick with formulas for how to do it. Somewhere in all that strategizing, we ought to send every school a twenty-foot banner to hang on the third-floor window (or stretch above the entryway). In eight-foot-high letters it would call for CONVERSATION. Not chat; conversation: time and colleagues and things that matter. It would give teaching a "certain thickness."

3

From the Bones Out

Teaching the Elements of Immersion Journalism

Kelly Peacock Wright and Carol Kuhl Barry

Coming back from Lee Gutkind's seminar on immersion journalism, we knew what it was like to be students—to be tossed out into an unfamiliar city, asked to find a story, and to return the next day with a quick-witted, finely crafted piece. We knew we wanted students who would own that kind of closely observed writing because they were curious, thoughtful, and determined.

We could sense the match between middle-school students and immersion journalism. We knew middle-school students inside out. We knew that routines are important, but so are choice, excitement, and variety. The reality of immersion journalism would guarantee that the work would never be described by that most dangerous of middle-school terms, "boring." We knew our students would jump at the chance to write outside the classroom, and we trusted that the cliffs and shores, mountains, and local history of San Diego and La Jolla would spark the "show, not tell" writing we were always hawking. On the other hand, we knew middle-school students need to be in carefully constructed but open-ended situations. And we knew that strong pieces of immersion journalism demanded absolute attention to research, reflection, and the craft of writing. How was that going to happen for our students, who had to be anywhere from prodded to dragged through a second draft?

The *we* that has appeared throughout these opening paragraphs is not an accident or a casual convention. Luckily, from the first morning in Cambridge right through to the last moments of binding our students' work, we had the luck and the privilege of working as a pair. So when this question of *how* loomed in front of us, neither one of us was alone.

Once we tapped that sense of partnership, we were free to realize that our possibilities were limitless. We began to list all the individuals and places and experiences that might serve as resources for student writers. We could see them observing, interviewing, and shadowing. The local newspaper, the museum, the historical society, the Pacific coast, and the tide pools all became possible writing prompts. We could imagine whole-group expeditions and walking tours for smaller groups of students. We saw a powerfully written collage about our community taking shape. We realized there was no reason to stick to recent history. Together, we could cross the border into social studies and connect with our investigations of ancient indigenous communities. And why not include predictions about the future? The students would do more than write. They could draw, sketch, even take photos. The sky was the limit. We had multiple entry points, we had choice, we had integration.

Then we put our heads up. Our students were eleven- and twelve-year-olds. We couldn't send them out to roam as we had done in Cambridge. We shuddered to imagine the scene where a sixth grader told his mother, "My teacher said I have to go to the mall by myself and wait for something to happen, then write about it." One-third of our students are bused from a much less affluent part of the city. La Jolla was not their community; would they feel safe? Interested? We thought about our local paper and our school library full of reference books. Where would we get current models of immersion journalism that would draw students in? Where would we get models that students could read and appreciate? How would we hold students' attention over the weeks and weeks it would take to craft a strong piece of journalistic writing?

Our earlier vision of steps leading up to a final product became even clearer. To guarantee that all of our students had an equal opportunity to be a part of this sustained process, we had to use school as a hub. At that hub we would provide the invitations and the questions to spark the expeditions, as well as the models, the conversation, and the editing to turn experiences into writing. Our block scheduling would allow for our expeditions and writing seminars. Because there were two of us, one could venture out with a smaller group of students while the other stayed "home" to work on writing. But most important was our original insight. This journalistic apprenticeship had to have clear steps. And each step had to be engaging in and of itself. Each step had to yield a satisfying piece of writing. And students had to see how each step was linked to a larger vision.

So we made a backbone for our project. We thought back to the seminar in Cambridge, asking ourselves what the elements were that we wanted students to grasp. Our answers:

Reality/Specific Detail: This was the whole point of the expeditions we planned, and the tools of interviewing and observing that we planned to teach. Students would be coming face to face with the community that, up until then, many of them just walked through or lived in. We were after close encounters, detail, and specificity.

Reflection/Theme: Students need to have a main point or focus to their work that communicates there is a thinking process involved, a message given, and some genuine reflection. Everything in the piece should be connected to that focus.

Research/Teaching Element: We were going to meet with individuals, read the history of the region, look at maps, etc. Students had to have something to say, not just ways of saying it.

'Riting/Craft: We were not interested in the same old "and then . . . and then" writing. We were after more:

A story structure: We wanted a dramatic beginning or lead; a question or mystery worth tracking; a high point.

Scenes: We wanted students to capture the immediacy of being in a particular time and place, at a very specific moment. And we wanted those scenes to build up, leading one to another.

Voice/Tone: We wanted the pieces to communicate the sense of a particular individual taking in information and making sense of what was experienced, but subtly, without the steady beat of "I saw . . . I learned . . . I thought . . ."

We had the makings of a remarkable idea. The final challenge was to get the architecture of the unit right. We wanted a careful staircase leading students to a place where they could take on the demands of immersion journalism. That meant chances to:

1. *Write a comparison/contrast essay.* Students will research life for the indigenous population of our region up to the nineteenth century, then compare/contrast it with life in La Jolla today.
2. *Compose original poetry.* Students may choose between two types of poetry: found poetry, using excerpts taken from memoirs of La Jolla residents; and narrative poetry, using information gained from research, observations, and/or interviews.
3. *Conduct interviews.* Students will write questions designed to gather data. They will present their information as ethnographers. Students will use this information for several pieces such as feature stories, editorials, and poetry.
4. *Write a feature story.* Students will immerse themselves in creative nonfiction. They will bring to life the people, sights, and sounds of La Jolla.
5. *Write editorials.* Students will make decisions about what problems are on the minds of La Jolla's residents or visitors. Students may decide to identify a particular problem themselves, then offer a solution.
6. *Write a narrative.* Students will compose stories written from the point of view of a native: Native American, or native La Jollan. "A Day in the Life of" will be the format. Students will compose stories in the first person to portray themselves as residents of or visitors to La Jolla.
7. *Write observational essays.* Students will choose to compose pieces from a particular point of view, either their own or an unusual one (like that of an inanimate object). The topics will include the people and areas in the vicinity of the school.

Artistic Products

1. *Photography.* Students will capture life in the village as it is today and compare and contrast it to life as it was in days gone by using photos provided by the historical society.
2. *Watercolor.* Students will produce original watercolors of the sights in and around the village and beach.
3. *Sketching.* Students will create original sketches of the sights in and around the village and beach. Students will engage in minute observational drawing with the aid of a jeweler's loupe.

The next step was to go public. We notified the parents of our plans to do the project and inquired about their ability to help:

Dear Parents,

Beginning the week of March 20th, and continuing through May, the Language Arts classes of Mrs. Barry and Mrs. Wright will be engrossed in a very special writing project.

The project, which culminates in the production of a book, will focus on the area in and around La Jolla as it was in ancient history, as it exists today, and as it may become in the future. Students, with information gained through observation, interview, research, and special presentations, will write narratives, poems, editorials, and feature stories. They will also have the opportunity to create original works of art that will illustrate the publication.

To ensure that this project will be a success, the students will be taking a series of walking trips to the village, the beach, and Mt. Soledad to make observations, take notes, and sketch. Parent volunteers for the walking trips would be greatly appreciated.

If there is time available in your schedule to chaperone a small group of students for one or more walking trips, or if you have information that is pertinent to this project, such as photographs, artifacts, or knowledge that you might share with students, please let us know by returning the slip below. Thank you in advance for your interest in this great endeavor.

Sincerely,
Kelly Peacock Wright & Carol Barry

We then designed our second piece of architecture, a basic framework for each writing lesson:

1. Provide at least two good models of the genre.
2. Students develop generalizations from exemplars, then make a chart to use as a reference and help guide writing.
3. Provide a graphic organizer to give a visual of the big idea.
4. Provide guided practice in class and at home to give experience.
5. Students then write a piece in response to a final writing prompt and use the extracted criteria/generalization chart to peer-edit pieces, and construct a scoring rubric if needed.

If we used this framework consistently, it would provide the students with a sense of growing familiarity and involvement because they would be investigating, discovering, making connections, and using their knowledge to write in the same genre they had been reading.

As planned, we offered our students a variety of professional and student-authored pieces as exemplars. Some of these pieces were collected specifically for this project, and others from past students over many years. We used the student-authored pieces along with the collected professional and published pieces to assist students in understanding what "makes a horse a horse," or in each case, what elements make up a piece of poetry, an observational essay, or a feature story.

In addition to articulating common criteria for each piece, we asked our students to assess what made particular pieces better or stronger examples of the genre. The students read and examined an exemplar, and inferred the criteria used to develop and write a piece in that particular genre. The criteria extracted from these exemplars became not only the basis for developing students' own instances of a particular genre of writing, but also the scoring guide for the writing assignment.

A First Step: Writing Editorials

Before the first field trip, students composed editorials about controversial issues in La Jolla/San Diego. We began there in part because we had strong exemplars. Also, any editorial demands a unifying point.

In their editorials, students presented their points of view and took the opportunity to interview their parents. They wrote about topics as varied as the deplorable traffic conditions in La Jolla and pollution in the coastal waters.

Students certainly began to practice point of view and tone, as the following pieces show.

La Jolla Water Pollution

I think water pollution in La Jolla is worse than some people think. It affects everyone in some way. You can even catch hepatitis from the water, which could kill you.

My friends and I are always getting sick from the water because we surf. One of my friends had to get an infection removed from his arm from the dirty water. He was out of the water for half the summer.

It makes me so mad to walk to the beach and see "Keep Out" signs all over. Every time it rains we have to stay out of the water for about three days. When it rains, oil, fertilizer, pesticides, and many other chemicals and wastes are flushed down straight into the ocean.

I don't know how to stop the problem, but if everyone helped and watched what they threw in the storm drains, watched what they put in their gardens and spilled in the street, we would be on the way to clean water, a healthy sea, animals and surfers.

Andrew Farnsley

Several students chose to write editorials about Mt. Soledad, a focus of controversy in recent times. A Christian cross sits on public land there and is viewed by some as interfering with rights guaranteed by the U.S. Constitution. The following excerpt showcases one student's opinion and incorporates a strong point of view and distinct tone.

. . . So what about the division of church and state? To me, there's no such thing! The Constitution was written by our

> forefathers. They based it on the Bible and God. Now you're telling me the very people who built this country were wrong, and because they're long gone and dead now, that we can ignore the laws and regulations they set up? I think not. Tell me again. What do all the presidents put their hands on while being sworn in? What do witnesses in trials have to put their hands on, and who's supposed to help them tell the truth and nothing but the truth? One nation under who? The Victoria what? What shape is that medal of honor in? I could fill up a whole page with these sorts of contradictions and double standards. I believe there is a rule. It should be applied in every circumstance that it can. No one should be able to pick and choose, and if someone is able to apply it selectively, then it isn't really a rule . . .
>
> *Patrick Klima*

Although many students were able to write an editorial with all of the necessary components, others, not seeming to care about such impersonal topics, completed the assignment but without a distinct voice. We had failed to consider an important point: that middle-school students are often obsessed with the notion of fairness. We assumed that allowing students to choose their own topic was "fair." But our students often remind us that true choice means that they can choose not only their topic, but the style in which they write about it. This process was as much about our learning to improve the opportunities we offer our students as it was about our students improving their writing.

Finally, the day of the first field trip arrived. With it came another chance to think about point of view—from a very different vantage point. The walking trip to the observation point at the top of Mt. Soledad provided the students with another approach and point of view from the editorials they had just written. It gave them a chance to think about physical point of view through observation.

In class we talked about the idea of personification and about a writer's omniscient point of view, often described as being "Godlike." We also asked students to "speculate on the activities of the people below as they go about their daily lives. Do they seem important, or insignificant, from this height? Why? How does this experience compare or contrast with the omniscient or third-person point of view in a story? Do you have an 'all-knowing' feeling from where you stand?"

Students used their mountaintop observations, whether written down or simply experienced, to write an observational essay. To our delight, many of the pieces gave the feeling that "someone was talking," and demonstrated "show, not tell" (yes, they had learned that!). And many students who had been nearly impossible to motivate throughout the year not only completed the essay, but excitedly discussed it. The experience had been worthwhile. Students who had never had anything to show became known as capable writers.

> In the weeks since I've been to Mount Soledad, I have been wondering—if this place could have feelings and speak, what would it tell me? I've thought about it and I think that if it could do any of those things, it would tell me that it is a peaceful place. Many people visit just for the view. It might tell me that it is angry that some people want to take the cross down. Without the cross, Mount Soledad is just a plain, old hill. It might say that so many animals scurry over it, that it tickles!
>
> *Karlye Christensen*

> From the mountain I look off into the distance, stretching the boundaries from which my eyes can see. The low mist and clouds veil the mountains with a translucent curtain, hiding the mountains, afraid to be seen. Ridges and peaks are pulled up out of the ground by the merciless grasp of the sky.
>
> My eyes climb up into the air, but are stopped from seeing any further by heavily spread grayish blue clouds—each one outlined with a dull silver lining and shadowed by the cloud next to it, giving off a mystical look and feel. It's comforting to see the sleepy clouds sagging over the sky like drowsy eyelids. Somehow it is quite satisfying.
>
> *Amy Reed*

The colors are bright and vivid, and then all of a sudden fade as the distance becomes greater. The wind rustles through the chaparral making the whole effect of the clouds seem to come to life.

Nicole Oncina

While atop Mt. Soledad, the students also wrote poetry. The structured style of haiku provided a demanding but creative "container" for students' observations, feelings, and personal points of view.

Mt. Soledad
Morning at the cross
A jet streaks above our heads
Nothing left behind
Zach Austin

Clouds
Clouds in my backyard
Flying dragons, sailing ships
A kite with streamers
Zach Austin

From Perspective to Scenes

To illustrate another element of creative nonfiction, scenes in a series, we shared reprints of personal memoirs written by long-time residents of La Jolla. The autobiographical pieces recounted the "golden days" of the town when, as adolescents, the writers spent the days of summer with friends on the tennis courts, or lounging near the cove. Students used details and phrases from these stories to construct "found" poetry. Students arranged the words or phrases to capture the essence of the text or create a new scene.

La Jolla
The golden years of the village
culture and recreation
A small slice of middle America

Typical, but very intense
Expensive days spent laughing about nothing.

Amy Reed

Summer Days
The golden hills charm, days passed at the cove
Vivid memories of joy this gave me
I would treasure this gift forever
A so-called twinkle at the shores
Lights dancing in the distance
Evenings of isolation and solitary thinking
Appreciate the quiet
Night beauty stars
Drifting clouds
Crackling fire
A sometimes florescent ocean . . .

Amy Reed

Students even used the techniques of "found poetry" to transform the prose of a La Jolla Historical Society publication into this more lively piece:

> "The Major" was one of our favorite La Jolla characters, whose charming manner and eccentricities delighted us all. No matter that it was whispered that he had a silver plate in his head. When not on the courts, he was often found at the Cove, sitting in his overstuffed armchair at water's edge, cooling feet and ankles in the surf, surrounded by adoring children.
>
> Much later, the Major took a wife, a hillbilly type with golden curls and sunny disposition, always barefoot, and, as I remember, always pregnant. I recall seeing them drive away on their honeymoon to Mexico in a pickup truck, their belongings packed into three shiny new large galvanized garbage pails that gleamed in the sun of their happy departure.

In much less space, a student was able to sum this up quite nicely:

Hillbilly
Golden curls,
Sunny disposition,
Always barefoot,
Always pregnant
Honeymoon,
Truck,
Happy departure.

Raphael Chejade-Bloom

Research: The Fine Art of Finding Out

The work of choosing and arranging details to make a point is far from simple—it escapes many adults. So in order to prepare our students to immerse themselves in a situation later, we gave them another opportunity to sit and carefully observe a scene or an object. To develop their observational skills, students drew a close-up of an object taken from nature using a jeweler's loupe. This activity, borrowed from a Seattle project entitled "Private Eye," asked students to draw a magnified section of an object exactly as it appeared. We specifically asked them not to interpret what they were seeing. After drawing a section of these objects, students wrote metaphors to describe their drawings (Figure 3–1). This activity really began to knit together careful observation, perspective, and point of view. We had clearly left the realm of individual skills, practiced in isolation.

So we were ready to add in research. One important aspect of immersion journalism is the inclusion of conversation or dialogue taken from individuals being observed. Earlier in the year, students had interviewed their grandparents and written firsthand biographies. They had learned to ask questions and to conduct an interview to obtain specific information. Their work was engaging and full of voice, but in many cases the resulting pieces were simply a series of questions with responses. In completing the immersion journalism project, students again conducted interviews to gather information, and then used that information to compose a piece of creative nonfiction. We wondered whether they would

FIGURE 3–1. *Private Eye Drawings by Daniel Kruger*

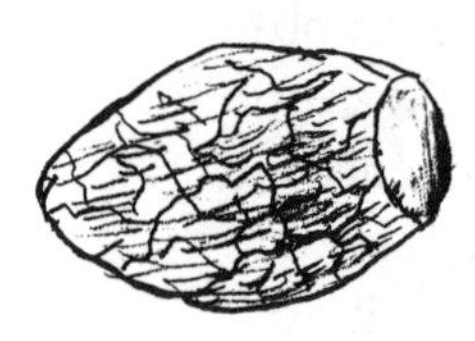

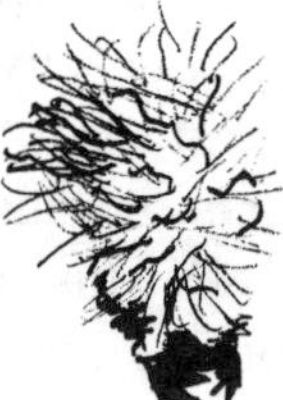

FIGURE 3–1. (*cont.*)

This looks like a spaceship going through the atmosphere, and the heat has caused it to burst up in flames as it drops to the earth's ocean

This looks like a cat's paw grabbing a humungous coffee bean

This looks like a bunch of pyramids reaching to the sky like skyscrapers.

This looks like a black terrior walking on sticks in the forest

This looks like the hands of someone with long nails presenting some snacks to someone. the snacks are in a bowl.

This looks like a porcupine's back.

remember the past experience sufficiently in order to go beyond mere question-response. We were asking them to reach way back.

Bringing the Elements Together

Up to this point, students had practiced the elements of what Lee Gutkind called the architecture of an essay: story structure, scene, voice/tone, detail, and research. In writing a feature story, students would need to *combine* all of these elements into one piece. The students would be expected to immerse themselves in a situation of their own choosing and construct a feature story or a creative nonfiction essay. It was time to find out whether all they had learned would be remembered and retrieved to write a final immersion journalism project.

To introduce the genre of creative nonfiction to students, we first read a number of published feature stories in class. We chose feature stories because they were available in the newspapers we received in class, and because we had many good pieces saved from a variety of other sources. (The difficulty with choosing exemplars was readability level. A number of excellent pieces that we considered had to be excluded because they were too difficult for the students.) After discussing the exemplars we finally chose, students were asked to think about the criteria or elements of a feature story. We found our sixth graders were just as insightful as the adult participants in our curriculum seminar had been. Students then looked for feature stories in local newspapers. Stories were easy to find; the more difficult problem was locating ones that were interesting and relevant to this age group.

Our original fear of not having time to find the range of appropriate exemplars we wanted to have on hand had come to haunt us. But together we found another way to help students see how connected all the parts are in powerful pieces of creative nonfiction. We read aloud from Jim Trelease's book, *Read All About It*—but only the leads. The students were then asked if they wanted to hear the rest: "Are you hooked?" Yes, they were, and the stories were finished. There were elements of plot, specific points of view, distinct voices heard, some dialogue, and, most importantly, a strong theme. The pieces had begun with a true event, but had been altered somewhat by the author to build in the elements that may normally be missing from a true feature story, but are evident in a piece of immersion journalism. There was the seamless quality students would need to keep in mind as they approached the task of writing their own feature stories.

We developed a guide to serve a dual purpose: to help students identify the common elements in the feature stories found in the newspaper, and to aid them in writing their own (Figure 3–2). Students also used it later to critique and assess one another's creative nonfiction (Figure 3–3).

It was time to venture out and write creative nonfiction. Students each chose a topic that had some connection to La Jolla: restaurants, the Beach and Tennis Club, the cove, the caves, the Dieguenos (a group indigenous to the area), or prominent local figures. Students returned to sketching sights. They visited places on their own and wrote observational pieces. After their initial observations, students thought of an angle or slant for their article. In follow-up visits students could reflect about what they had observed and revise their earlier efforts.

Earlier drafts often featured one or another key element. For example, in the following feature story Meggie Hai "finds" an important theme—but not until the conclusion:

Feature Story—The Dieguenos

Have you ever thought that years ago someone might have lived on the land that your house sits over? Well, that might be so. A long time ago before the settlers came, a Native American tribe lived on the land of San Diego. They were called the Dieguenos. They lived near what is now San Ysidro along the coast. For my interview, I researched the interview of a Diegueno named Delfina Cuero. The following is the background of the Dieguenos.

The Dieguenos had a plentiful diet. They were hunter-gatherers. The men hunted, the women gathered. From the ocean, they got abalone, shellfish, starfish, scallop, crab, lobster, fish, shrimp, octopus, and clams. They gathered salt

FIGURE 3–2. *Creative Nonfiction Common Element Guide*

Creative Nonfiction
Architecture of an Essay
Common Elements

Name ____________________
Date ____________________

Symbolic Theme
What is the focus or message of the piece?

____
____
____
____
____

Dialogue
How is dialogue used in the piece? What is the effect?

____
____
____
____
____

Lead
How does the piece begin? What is the effect?

____
____
____
____
____

Teaching Element
What facts do you learn? How are they woven into the story?

____
____
____
____
____

Voice/Tone
Explain the voice or tone of the piece. What is the effect?

____
____
____
____
____

FIGURE 3–3. *Students' Creative Nonfiction Scoring Guide*

Name ______________________

FEATURE STORY
SCORING GUIDE

After reading many different feature stories, we, as a class, decided that a good feature story would contain the elements listed below. Comment on how you believe your piece demonstrates these important elements. Rate each of the elements for your piece on a scale of one to six, six being the top score.

Symbolic Theme (6 5 4 3 2 1)
Describe the focus or message of the piece.

____
____
____

Dialogue (6 5 4 3 2 1)
Is dialogue used in the piece? Why or why not, and what is the effect?

____
____
____

Lead (6 5 4 3 2 1)
How did you "grab" the attention of the reader?

____
____
____

Teaching Element (6 5 4 3 2 1)
How are the facts or teaching elements woven into the story?

____
____
____

Voice/Tone (6 5 4 3 2 1)
Explain the voice or tone of the piece. What is the effect?

____
____
____

from San Diego Bay to preserve meat. From the woods they got wild cherries, wild wheat, honey, greens, acorns, pine nuts, and hunted rabbits. They also ate cactus, deer, opossum, raccoon, wood rat, and cotton tail rabbit. They made flour out of wild cherries, acorns, lilacs, and other flowers. They also made traps, nets, boats, and fish spears out of reed, agave, grass, and cactus thorns.

When doing this Feature Story, I learned a lot about the Native American tribes that used to live here. I too hope that my story will serve as a reference. The reason that Delfina did this interview is because she wants to answer the question, "Is there room for us in America? Can we come home legally?" I feel that sometimes we have to ask this question ourselves. In the future, Americans should try to pay the Native Americans for the land that they stole.

Meggie Hai

Here a young writer has mastered the inclusion of information and lively quotes:

The La Jolla Caves

This is where the history of La Jolla first began. It is still a main tourist attraction and was made by nature. It took nature thousands of years to create these natural wonders, and they are still just as interesting today. Today, they still remain part of the Shell Shop.

The founder of the cave is unknown. Two years of hard work by a German professor from 1902–1903, while using a pick and shovel, built the first staircase to the lighted tunnel of Sunny Jim. The cave was then given away to the American public by the professor.

"This cave has been used by movie producers as settings and backgrounds," said a worker at the shop. "It has also been rated by magazines and Encyclopedia Americana as a 'must see' sight in Southern California. Each day we have about eighty to one hundred people come in, wanting to go down into Sunny Jim. It's a real tourist attraction."

Aramara Garcia

In the following excerpt, Jed has evidence of necessary research, the use of quotations, as well as detailed observation.

The Children's Pool: An Historical Landmark

A long time ago a wonderful woman named Ellen Browning Scripps had a dream. She dreamed of a way to keep both children and adults safe from the ocean's mighty power. From her dream the Children's Pool was constructed.

On May 31, 1931, Judge J. T. Dean said, "This is the most valuable of all of Mrs. Scripps' benefits to La Jolla, measured in terms of good to the greatest number were those investments in human happiness designed for the little ones." D. C. Harper added, "Adults must recognize that here at the pool the children have primary claim."

To the south of the Children's Pool the bluffs are very steep and high. To the north of the pool the La Jolla Shores beaches are long and sandy and make the best place to get tan and go swimming. Not too far from the beaches Mt. Soledad rises 808.3 feet. In 1887, Mt. Soledad was described as the gentle sloping hill back of La Jolla covered with native vegetation. It is an attractive feature, the incline of the mountain is just enough for a healthy climb to the top.

The Children's Pool is a wonderful place to go and spend the day, except if you're planning to spend the day there swimming. If you are planning on that, a good place to go is the La Jolla Shores beaches. The waves are not big and there are no sea lions to watch out for. Plus, there is a bigger beach and more lifeguards. Even though you may be safer at the Shores, the Children's Pool is a gift to be enjoyed for many generations.

Jed Walsh

The lead of the following piece shows how to get a reader's attention in a creative fashion.

The La Jolla Playhouse

Murder, romance, comedy, suspense: where in La Jolla can you go to find all this? The La Jolla Playhouse of course. Since 1947 people from all over the world have been coming to La Jolla to be entertained at the Playhouse. Some of the best actors and directors in the world have worked there.

Back when the Playhouse was started, they did not have a fancy stage like they do now. The plays were performed on the La Jolla High School stage. The first play that was ever given at the Playhouse was "Night Must Fall." The actors who were involved with the Playhouse were Gregory Peck, Dorothy McGuire, and Mel Ferrer, who were famous actors back then. La Jolla was a much smaller community then and the La Jolla High School theater was big enough. But even in those days, the word spread about the Playhouse, and people started coming from other places to see the plays.

Zach Austin

We took stock: although students were able to produce feature stories, including a variety of the elements that they had identified in feature stories themselves, they were missing the essential *combination* of all that was necessary to create a strong piece of immersion journalism. Would it *ever* happen?

A Day at the Cove

In the homestretch of the project, we spent a last day at the Cove. While two of the four groups walked to the Cove to sketch and read their original poems, gathering ideas for their own feature stories, the remaining groups had the opportunity to walk into the village to visit a restaurant with a spectacular view of the coastline. The students were to listen to a speaker from the La Jolla Historical Society present information about La Jolla's early days. The presentation held their attention periodically, but did not seem to truly interest them. This was something we had observed before and was showing itself to be true again. We were now certain that expecting sixth graders to capture a moment was more than difficult—unless it was *their* moment.

From the restaurant, the students descended to Ellen B. Scripps Park, situated above the Cove, to observe and write. At least outside, they had nature, people, and each other from which to draw material. And they had an assignment sheet. The students were instructed to use anything of personal interest from the beginning of the walking trip until their arrival back at school to construct a feature story. For most of the students, the writing originated from their observations in the park, most likely due to the sheet of paper they were given to record observations and a possible "slant."

The following piece of student writing represents the culmination of two months of work: a series of assignments designed to provide them with increasing opportunity to discover the necessary elements of a creative nonfiction work in other styles of writing.

This example most closely captures the essence of a controlling theme in a completed work. Again, what stands out is that this immediacy comes from a piece of research where *the author* chooses the topic. Interestingly, not just Erin but several others tracked the same subject.

A Step Too Far

With our eyes glued to the girl, she slipped beneath the splintered wooden rails that kept curious children away from the edges of the cliffs. Maybe we were just too curious for those gates to hold us back or maybe we just had to, but some of us slipped through after her, stalking her as a fox does a rabbit, ready to pounce any moment, or in this case, make a run for it.

We had all been sitting scattered around, but somewhat close to each other absorbing the peace, chatting and partially paying attention to our assignment, a project where we were to observe and write. No one had any particularly interesting thing to notice and observe, so we all just sat there, inhaling the salty wind and letting the breeze rustle through our hair, letting each strand dance in the air. We all just sat there—inhale, observe, write, exhale, inhale, observe, write, exhale . . . when someone interesting showed up. A girl, an idol, it didn't matter—she was cool. She wasn't one of the old people who came to relax and read, or one of the babies that came with their nannies to stretch their legs. It was simple, she was just cool. Too cool to be bothered with little sixth graders like us.

Her coarse bleached hair was chopped to show off the many earrings that lived in her ear. The rings that occupied her nose and eyebrow glittered in the afternoon sun like stars in a dark night. Her cool weirdo friends swarmed around her like busy bees worshipping their queen. So while we pretended to work silently, we secretly eyed her, cautiously, casually following her with eagerness, all hoping to be approved of. When we saw her slip under the fence and head down the cliffs, we were sick of just watching her, and I guess it was Veronica who decided to start some action.

Quietly, carefully, and daringly, someone puts one foot over the wooden beam, then the other, looking around to see if anyone was watching her besides the excited group of girls behind her cheering her on. There is already one other person from our group following the cool girl down the cliff, but unlike this girl, she took a running leap and wildly hurled over the crooked fence, missing the rigid edge of the cliff only by a few meters. The cool girl had already disappeared from sight, descending down the perilous cliffs. Some people pleaded with our wild friend not to go any further, but some urged her on. We all watched them tensely, wondering if we should go accompany our two friends on the other side of the fence.

"Come back."

"No, go on. Wait for me. What's up there?"

Different voices argued over what she should do. These voices argued over what was going to happen, what movie this reminded them of, what title the newspaper would hold tomorrow and on and on. Despite the commotion behind her, Veronica doesn't budge, or even say a word—at least not to us. She starts jabbering on and on to the cool girl, ruining our act of trying to be cool. The girl starts to walk up the cliff. Soon she is joined by her friends. One, I noticed, looked especially strong. We all decided it was time to back off then. It was then we realized what we were fooling with them and how they came to do something that had nothing to do with us. We stepped off their ground and decided it was time to just play the role of ourselves.

I thought of something that I learned from this experience that is pretty important. We all were looking across a border when we were looking at the girl, but what border was it? Obviously it was a fence to keep us out as curious children so we wouldn't go off the cliff, but there was another fence we were looking over that day, and the girl and us were looking across it. The truth is, the girl went down the cliff to smoke—not your everyday cowboy cigarette, but the real life-destructing thing. She was once curious too, like us, looking across the fence to the cliffs, and like us she was too curious for the fence to hold her back, so she went through. The only difference is that she crossed a much different fence than us. You could say she crossed the fence of morality, but every step she takes closer to the edge the more daring she will feel to go farther, and soon, no one will know how long it will take, but eventually she will lose her grip and fall off.

There are many fences in our lives that we should try to avoid, but there are often people on the other side to tempt us. I think the fence is made out of our morals, and when we don't have certain morals we are free to explore places that are dangerous. We all ought to stay on our own side of the fence, and stay with our own morals, not following other people, because you never know where the cliff ends or when the ground will crumple away beneath you.

Erin Glass

Had this whole project been a worthwhile experience for the students? The majority of the students had success with some of the segments that led toward the final piece, but had difficulty capturing the essence of a true piece of immersion journalism by including *every* element of that genre in a particular piece. But, as teachers, we are convinced that expectations are everything. Students will rise to meet the expectations we set for them. With that in mind, we set high expectations not only for our students, but for ourselves as well. Our initial list of project objectives clearly shows that we had set out to accomplish something quite grand.

In this first round, what we found was this: the lessons provided in class to prepare the students for that final experience proved to be more valuable than the end product. It is those episodes of learning that the students will take with them as they write for other purposes in later grades. That is what makes the experience of teaching challenging curriculum like immersion journalism so important. As educators, we need to think more often of two critical issues: first, we must provide multiple opportunities to complete skill-oriented tasks that build toward a greater product; and second, we must make sure that those tasks are rich in and of themselves.

Thinking in a forward fashion, this is a project that ought to span all the middle-school years. Students need the time to grow into the expectations that this kind of writing demands. Teachers can look closely at what is involved to provide many successful opportunities throughout each year in order to get an exemplary piece of immersion journalism by the end of a student's eighth-grade year.

Students at this age more than any other must have a reason to produce meaningful work. Most of what they are asked to do is within the confines of a classroom from information taken out of a book, and largely outside of their control. Immersion journalism offers students the opportunity to learn through experience. Middle-level students thrive when they are asked to do anything based on their own experiences. Their unique points of view and desire to be heard establish a natural platform from which they can leap into immersion journalism. They need time to grow as writers. One year is not enough to create the ultimate result. It is, however, ample time to begin the process.

References

Trelease, Jim. 1993. *Read All About It! Great Stories, Poems, and Newspaper Pieces for Reading Aloud for Preteens and Teens.* New York: Viking Penguin.

Reflections from a Colleague

Dennie Palmer Wolf

Spread out on the table in front of us were stacks of student writing. Maybe even heaps. We had a precious hour to decide which pieces made the best illustrations for Kelly Peacock Wright and Carol Kuhl Barry's chapter for this book. I just listened: "I think . . . What if . . . This has a great beginning but it just dies before the end. . . . The questions in this one . . . She really figured out about endings . . . Did you see what he finally did with the image of the mountain . . . ?" Then with that crazy end-of-day humor Kelly said, "I know, take the best from each one . . ." And Carol replied," . . . and print just one huge perfect piece."

That image of the one great journalism piece in the sky was right. Here were two teachers who went out on their own journalism expedition together, who hunted for materials together, who were brave enough to write together—not as a one-two pair, but elbow to elbow. As the afternoon wore on, Carol put Meggie Hai's piece on the Dieguenos into the middle of the table: "See, this is what I was teaching. I really wanted my kids to come out of this capable of writing a feature story. I wanted them to do a piece that was pulled along by the need to answer a question, to get to the heart of something by asking questions."

Kelly nodded toward a stack of papers from the final day at the beach. She read aloud a few sentences from Erin Glass's portrait of an older girl:

> A girl, an idol, it didn't matter—she was cool. She wasn't one of the old people who came to relax and read, or one of the babies that came with their nannies to stretch their legs. It was simple, she was just cool. . . . Her coarse bleached hair

> was chopped to show off the many earrings that lived in her ear. The rings that occupied her nose and eyebrow glittered in the afternoon sun like stars in a dark night. Her cool weirdo friends swarmed around her like busy bees worshipping their queen.

"And see, that is what I was after, that feeling of being in the presence of something. The fascination . . ." She paused. "It's interesting, in the end, we each had half of it. . . . That's what the chapter is all about . . . now I realize . . . it took us both a semester to get our half right. Now we want to take all three years of middle school and teach it some each year so we can get the whole thing to come together." Carol listened to Kelly, then pushed the Dieguenos piece up to meet the portrait of the older girl. "Like that."

Team-teaching can have the flavor of "I'll do the literature, you do the social studies." But this way of working was quite different. It was more like "joined teaching" or "twinned teaching." Both Carol and Kelly started out to do the "same" thing—they shared planning, field trips, materials. But they taught to different ends, different home plates. Carol headed toward investigation, Kelly toward encounter.

"So?" you say. "What's new?" Yes, of course, a teacher gives a flavor or a slant. But that's not what Carol and Kelly were seeing. No, sitting with all their student work, they saw the complementarity of what they had done—that each had half by the tail. And that it would take all of middle school to cross investigation with encounter to get immersion journalism. With that, sixth, seventh, and eighth grade blur. They become an arc.

4

Immigrant Education

Using Immersion Journalism to Expand the Teaching of English as a Second Language

Linda Reilly

The invitation was simple and attractive: join a group of teachers for a curriculum workshop on a new approach to writing for middle-school students. The writing genre was immersion journalism, and the workshop would be led by writer and college professor Lee Gutkind. We would read, write, and plan together, and at the end of three days I would have a new unit to take back to my class of eighth-grade English to Speakers of Other Languages (ESOL) students. As an added inducement, I could trade in the gray days of December in Rochester, New York, for the bright lights and excitement of Cambridge and Boston. It would be fun—almost a vacation.

It was December when I found myself in Cambridge, on the first morning of the seminars. "And finally, here are your official reporter's notebooks. No self-respecting journalist would be caught without one! Good luck!" With these words, our resident immersion journalist Lee Gutkind prepared to send us off to Cambridge's Central Square for our first foray into immersion journalism.

The workshop was barely an hour old; I hadn't even finished my first cup of coffee. I glanced around the room at the other twelve teachers I had met only that morning. Sticking pens into the spiral bindings of their reporter's notebooks, they looked calm, comfortable, and ready to force themselves upon perfect strangers in Central Square.

"Wait!" I hoped the edge of panic wasn't noticeable to my fellow journalists. "Let me ask a hypothetical question. What if someone . . . doesn't want to do this? What if someone feels . . ." I searched for a grown-up sounding word.

". . . scared?" Lee finished my question.

I no longer remember whatever words of support and encouragement Lee offered. All I recall is an anxious walk down Massachusetts Avenue, and the solid reassurance of Woolworth's storefront in Central Square. Childhood memories reminded me that this was a place to feel at ease, and the steady stream of international men, women, and children walking through the doors represented the kind of people I knew I could talk with.

Once in the store, I searched for easy targets to practice on. A young boy knelt on the floor, mesmerized before the fish tanks. I tried to sound friendly as I asked about his purchase plans, but after his third monosyllabic reply, I realized with embarrassment that for the sake of a swift conclusion to my assignment, I was expecting this child to forget everything his parents had taught him and give me jewels of dialogue that I could incorporate into a scintillating essay. I hastily retreated to the clothing department, hoping that I had not been observed by any of the store's employees.

In the women's department, the friendly, open chatter of women from Jamaica, China, and Ukraine drew me effortlessly into a successful immersion experience, which I was able to capture during our writing session:

> Standing together at the clothes racks, we are all women united in the simple acts of carefully examining the pants, shirts, and nightgowns on display. We pull out items for inspection, and cast sidelong glances at each other's choices. Subtle movements of eyebrows and foreheads convey approval or rejection.
>
> "Do you know if there's a dressing room?" I ask my neighbor.
>
> "Dr—dr—drez . . . ?" she asks with heavily accented voice. "Drezzes?" She gestures vaguely toward another part of the store.

"Place to put on clothes," I say slowly, with accompanying pantomime.

"Oh, oh, no . . . I think no . . . You just buy," she says, and smiles in a supportive way.

By the end of the three-day workshop, I had moved from fear and anxiety to exhilaration. I celebrated the finished pieces of writing from two of my colleagues, but I was positively in love with my 100-word fragment. I had been immersed, and I had surfaced, not only still breathing, but energized.

A month later I sat at home planning an immersion journalism project for my class of intermediate-level eighth-grade ESOL students at Thomas Jefferson Middle School in Rochester, New York. In spite of the excitement of my own writing experience, I knew there would be challenges translating what I had learned into a meaningful experience for my students. Good immersion pieces are carefully crafted to present one unifying theme, "the rubber band pulling all the details into a main point of focus," as Lee told us. This genre is an up-close-and-personal kind of writing, packed with intimate details. The reader can just about smell, feel, and taste the subject. And you can certainly *hear* the subject, as immersion journalism pieces are full of dialogue.

This was sophisticated writing. Could my students jump into what Lee called "magic moment journalism"? They were struggling to put sentences together in a cohesive paragraph, and for some, the sentence itself was a challenge. I wanted to be sure that I could address the near-yearning my students had voiced many times: to read and write grammatically correct English. As Ngoc had so often demanded of me: "Mrs. Reilly, teach the 'I am's and 'you are's!"

In addition, immersion journalism required writers to get out into the world, to interact with people. If I was nervous about going to Central Square, how would my students feel about leaving the cocoon of our ESOL class to talk with strangers around the city? For some of the students, just talking with the cafeteria staff was a challenge:

> When I went for lunch I was lost and I did not know how to talk in English. I just walked around the hallway for many

> times, at last I saw a teacher and I asked her where is the lunch room, then she took me to the lunch. When I took lunch, the lady asked me the lunch ticket, I said I don't know and she hold me there. I was scaring and I did not know what is happening, then they showed me a ticket and asked, "Do you have this?" and I took it out.
>
> *Tuan Bui*

To better understand Tuan, I began reading Janet Bode's book *New Kids on the Block: Oral Histories of Immigrant Teens* with the idea of introducing these lively vignettes to my students. I knew I wouldn't have to coerce the students to read the excerpts from this engaging collection of personal essays. They too had struggled with cross-cultural challenges such as Von experienced in his new American school:

> There were no Vietnamese kids at the school, and only one Chinese boy, but he became my best friend. After a while I got along with the other students. I met a very nice black boy. He thought I was Chinese and all Chinese know karate and kung fu. He said, "I like your country's movies." I told him, "I'm Vietnamese." But he didn't know what was Vietnamese. He took me home to meet his mother, and, wow, did they have a big TV. He said, "What do you want? Food?" "Yeah." He made food for me and we ate and drank soda. I didn't understand what I was seeing. I couldn't answer his questions, but we understood each other.
>
> "Later I invited him to my house. I was doing the laundry, but I didn't know how to do laundry here. In Vietnam we use a brush to scrub it, then take it outside and hang it in the wind. I washed it by hand in the bathtub and left it to dry. Two, three days, and it was not dry! The boy went, "Von, what is this? Why don't you bring it to a laundromat?" He didn't know my family never had even seen a washing machine.

From the pages of *New Kids* came my inspiration: a project on immigrant education. I finally felt I had hit upon an idea that would allow me to incorporate the learning goals I had set for this unit. First and foremost, the project had to be interesting enough to transcend the frustrations and fears of writing in a second language. Next, I wanted to link personal experience with public communication—as the writers in *New Kids* had done—as a rationale for setting high standards for the written work. The teenage writers of *New Kids* had also brought to light another important fact: parents and other adults had played important roles in supporting and encouraging these students to succeed in their academic endeavors. I knew the same support network existed for my students and I wanted to tap into it. Finally, I was looking for a new way to stress the importance of learning strategies for students learning language and content at the same time. Instead of explicitly teaching these strategies (I had already done plenty of that), I would have them go out and look for the strategies, all as part of the immersion experience.

Like the teenage writers of *New Kids*, my students had also had many poignant experiences in schools in their native countries and in America. But I didn't want them merely to tell their story one more time. Could they put their stories into a wider context that included the experiences of other immigrants, for example, young children and adults? Could these investigations of other age groups become the immersion? By starting from the familiar (their own school experiences) and moving out toward a consideration of other people's experiences, the students could have a kind of safety net for their immersion. I also hoped that if I sent my students out to speak to and observe other English-language learners, they would begin to think about what really matters for learning another language and succeeding in school.

I immediately imagined these immigrant stories as a student-made book. I decided to ask each student to create a book of essays that would take them (and their readers) on a journey from educational experiences in their native countries, to their first days of school in America, to the lives of other immigrants. A book would let several pieces of work paint a complex picture, more interesting than a single essay.

We began by reading from *New Kids on the Block*. These children speak of the frustrations and disappointments as well as the thrills and triumphs of immigrant teens in American schools. Experiences such as Sook's first week of school in America were achingly familiar to my students:

> Pretty soon it was September and there was nothing I could do. I had to go to school. Alone. Just before we moved here, my dad had told me, "You have to promise that no matter where you are, you will always be Korean."
>
> "I will, I will," I answered. That day at school, though, he and mom couldn't help me. I had to do it by myself. I thought, I will be a proud and respectful Korean. But I was in Hell! Everyone was giving me strange looks. There were no other Koreans in school. The whole week I saw three other Asians, a Thai girl and two Chinese, but that was it. This was my junior year all over again. I'd just finished it and the American school decided I had to do it again. I thought, my life is over. I'll die if I don't go back to my country.

My students were amazed to see a whole book published to tell *their* story. The readings had an energizing effect on the students: everyone did their homework, and discussions were lively. *New Kids* legitimized my writing assignments and helped to create an important sense of audience in my student-writers' heads. Riding a wave of enthusiasm, I handed out the first two writing assignments: "School in My Native Country" and "My First Experience of School in America."

From their descriptions of school customs in their native countries, it was clear to me that my students had had almost no experience of self-directed learning. Often their motivation had come from a fearful respect for the teacher's power over his students.

> The teachers are not fair to all the students if the parents of the students have a lot money or those who are smart kids they put those kids in the front [row] and those aren't get good grade they put them way back the end of the table.
>
> *Ngoc Nguyen (Vietnam)*

> The teachers in my Eritrea were very strict. If one student acted like a fool, he or she would get whipped with a stick on their hands or someplace on their body. With ruler the teachers hit the students on their fingers. The teachers put a pen between the student's fingers and squeezed the fingers against each other. Sometimes the teachers made the students get on their knees on hot day for a long time.
>
> *Ermias Ogbeab (Eritrea)*

> Most of the teacher whipped the students, and when the student didn't listen, the teacher would send them to the principal. The principal pulled the students ears until their skin would come off.
>
> *Fatuma Salongo (Kenya)*

These vivid memories were a powerful contrast to our American emphasis on student-centered learning. It made me think differently about why, after having been in American schools for two to three years, my students still needed a lot of prodding to use the learning strategies and self-motivation of self-directed learners.

As the class shared their essays in peer-editing conferences and small-group readings, I underscored all glimmers of these strategies that surfaced in the essays. Writing about their first experiences of school in America, several students emphasized the power of a positive attitude in the face of daunting obstacles.

> . . . I was looking for any Pakistani or Indian students but there were none of them and after that I felt so bad. But later on, I said to myself that it is not going to work like that. Then I started making my new friends. My new friends are so helpful and nice to me.
>
> *Neelofer Jaffery*

> Every day I had a lot, a lot of homework. But now it wouldn't be a lot of work because now it would be easy for me. When I just came it was hard for me. Some of the things are hard now but as time passes I will find yesterday's work was easy.
>
> *Anna Yakimiv*

> . . . I feel very proud of myself because I worked very hard for anything I want to do. I think I'm very lucky because I had learned other languages beside my own language.
>
> *Truc Le*

With these first two essays completed, I began to introduce the basic characteristics of immersion journalism. "How could you tell an interesting story about immigrant students in American classrooms?" I asked them. Several students agreed with Phitsamai's observation: "I think to make something interesting to read, there must be some excitement, like a fight or some jokes that a kid had made." Anna's account of her first day of school in America, when she confused recess with dismissal, helped illustrate this point. As everyone headed out the door, Anna hurriedly began her walk home:

> When I got home, the first thing my mom asked me was, "How come you came home that early? You were supposed to come home at 3:30, but why did you come at 1:30?" I said, "Everybody left for home so I did too." I didn't know that they went outside. I thought that they went home. The teacher started worrying and called my sponsor house, my friend house and my house because they didn't know what happened . . . When they called my house I didn't even understand anything so I just listened to everything what they said and then I put the phone down.

For our first immersion experience, I had arranged for the class to visit a nearby elementary school that housed one of the city's LEAP programs for younger children. (LEAP is a sheltered English program for beginning ESOL students in the Rochester City School District.) My students would be observing classes of multilingual immigrant children in which English is the medium of instruction. Some students had attended classes in this school before coming to Jefferson, and some of them had younger brothers and sisters in the school. For their classroom observations, I wanted to focus the children's attention beyond fights and jokes. In small groups students brainstormed lists to answer two questions: "How do children learn English best?" and "What makes a good class for immigrants?" Their answers ranged from "Watch Barney" to "Label objects around the class" to "Take trips and have assemblies." With over forty-five suggestions on the two lists, the students now had a comprehensive checklist to assist them in their observations in other classrooms. The plans were set, and it was time to wade in—to put emerging independence, self-direction, and observation to work.

"Next week as part of our Immigrant Education project, we will be visiting LEAP classes at School No. 5." Some smiles quickly lit up around the room, but it was the knitted brows, widening eyes, and tense mouths that I related to. It was "Off to Central Square!" all over again. However, these students displayed no reluctance to voice their concerns.

"Do we have to *talk* to them?"

"Will we be going into classes *alone*?"

"*I'm* not going!"

I was not giving in to anxiety—theirs or mine. "You'll visit each class in teams of four or five. You'll take your brainstorming lists and look for evidence around the room. You'll also use a classroom observation form to write down what you see and hear in the class." Some relaxed, others were still not convinced.

"It's only elementary school," I offered. "You're so far beyond them. How hard can it be?" I was trying to allay their fears, but I also knew that for many of them, the anxieties would not go away until the immersion began.

On the morning of our visit I passed out clipboards and papers. There was a nervous silence in the room as students organized their papers and pens. I watched as they set off down the sidewalk, clutching their clipboards like talismans or shields, and I suddenly wondered if that was what Lee had seen when he sent us off to Central Square with our reporter's notebooks. At 11:00 A.M., we arrived in the school and I began escorting teams to their classrooms. Most students went into their assigned classes willingly, but a few had to be pried off door jambs and coaxed into the room.

It was a typical school day in that the unexpected had merrily danced into our carefully crafted plans. The music teacher needed to rehearse the second graders, and my students were sent to music class instead of the reading lesson that had been scheduled. At the door of the first-grade class, a custodian preceded us into the room with a bucket and mop. The classroom teacher pointed to a little table in the back of the room. "That's where your students will sit," the teacher explained, "but they'll have to wait a few minutes. Juan just got sick back there." With no time to wait myself, I left with another group as disinfectant stung the air and an ashen Juan was led out to the nurse's office.

In the fifth/sixth-grade classroom where I temporarily parked myself, the patience of the unflappable Ms. Silvio was being tested. A new student had arrived two days ahead of schedule, without the appropriate paperwork, and members of the family (mother, grandmother, and two siblings) were parked on the floor outside the classroom while the teacher waited for clearance from the office to admit the girl. A Spanish-speaking student was traveling back and forth between family and teacher to explain what was going on. The classroom telephone rang several times, apparently with information relevant to the situation. Throughout this whole episode, Ms. Silvio cheerfully plugged away at the morning's lesson: reading a book about the Vietnam War Memorial in Washington, D.C. It was clear that the students adored and respected her, and that they were used to the occasional interruptions that punctuated their lessons. My students also sensed Ms. Silvio's commitment to her students; Neelofer captured this feeling when she wrote:

> . . . The interesting thing I saw in Mrs. Silvio's class was when she was talking on the phone and the person on the other line was holding for a minute . . . she start asking the questions to the students. I thought she was not wasting time for students.

When the time came to return to Jefferson, I was in for a surprise. My fledgling reporters were now completely immersed, and many did not want to leave. In the kindergarten room, the reporters were sitting cross-legged among the five-year-olds listening to the story Ms. Perlet was reading. Not wanting to interrupt, I motioned quietly at the door for them to come out. Smiling sweetly, they shook their heads "no." From door to door, I received similar responses. With much the same diplomacy that it had taken to coax them into the rooms, I finally pried everyone out.

Following our visit to School No. 5, I asked students to write up their accounts of the classroom visits. They could refer to their classroom observation sheets (Figure 4–1). We had talked about incorporating dialogue into a writing piece, as part of what teachers sometimes call "show, not tell" writing, and what Lee calls "cinematic, 3-D writing." My students had written dialogue before in their plays and short stories, but immersion journalism calls for writing from the opposite side of the dialogue coin. Rather than *invent* interesting things for a character to say, immersion journalists must *listen for* and *record* the important pieces of conversation. As preparation for the visit to School No. 5, I had stressed that it was important to write down as much of the classroom conversation as they could, since you can never predict when a conversational gem will surface.

Yet, as I expected, these essays came back with little or no dialogue, only sluggish indirect quotations. I decided to ask the students to look at their notes and write only dialogue. From there, students worked with partners to figure out how to merge the chunks of dialogue into their essays. I was pleased when Fatuma called me over to show me a numbering system she had developed for revising her essay. She chose dialogue she wanted to include, coded it with a number, then marked the place for insertion in her essay with that number. I knew we were on the right track when she willingly edited out bits of narration in order to let the dialogue carry the story. One paragraph in Fatuma's first draft begins with "The teacher . . ." followed by six sentences all beginning with "She . . ." (Figure 4–2). Writing teachers often advise their students to vary their sentence structure, but this can be difficult for ESOL students who are just beginning to master the declarative sentence. When Fatuma let the dialogue carry the essay forward, sentence variety was the inevitable result (Figure 4–3). "This is much better," she exclaimed. "The first one was boring." I agreed.

During Anna's visit to Ms. Perlet's kindergarten room, she observed an exchange between teacher and students that caught her

FIGURE 4–1. *Anna Yakimiv's Classroom Observation Notes*

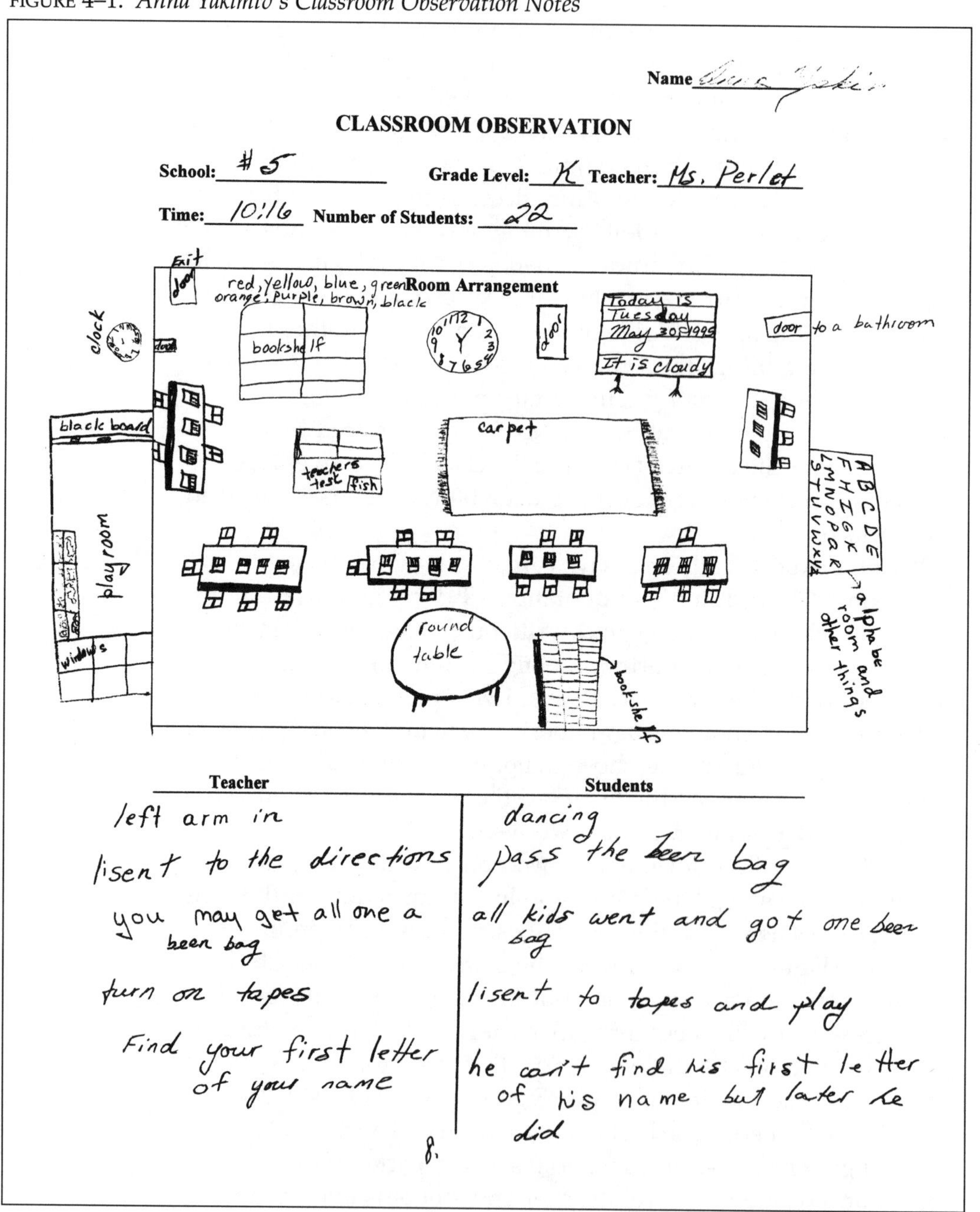

Name

CLASSROOM OBSERVATION

School: #5 Grade Level: K Teacher: Ms. Perlet

Time: 10:16 Number of Students: 22

Room Arrangement

Teacher	Students
left arm in	dancing
lisent to the directions	pass the been bag
you may get all one a been bag	all kids went and got one been bag
turn on tapes	lisent to tapes and play
Find your first letter of your name	he can't find his first letter of his name but later he did

8.

FIGURE 4–2. *Fatuma's First Draft*

Fatuma Salonge 5/31

When I first entered Mrs Silvio's class I saw students from different Countries.

Some Students were from Puerto Rico, Vietnam and other Countries. Many Students spoke English Pretty well and some spoke English a little. They answered every question that the teacher had ask them and they were noisy. They speak and whispered and made a lot of nois.

The teacher was nice to the students. She didn't yell at them all the time when they did something wrong. She told them to take out their books about the Vietnam War. She asked each student a question and they raised their hand. She even talked about the map of the Vietnam and asked one student about her Country. She walked around the class-room to make sure that each student are doing their work. She asked the Students about how do they feel when a person is teasing them about their countr and then she said "you kids learned a lot." "Very good"!

I Kind of liked the class, because the teacher was nice and I liked the way she taught the students.

FIGURE 4–3. *Finished Essay with Dialogue Included*

Mrs. Silvio's Class

When I first entered Mrs. Silvio's class, I saw students from different countries. We all stood up and introduced our selves. "What is your name?" "where are you from?" Mrs. Silvio said. Then she turned and started teaching class.

Some students were from Puerto Rico, Vietnam and other countries. Many students spoke English pretty well and some spoke English a little. They answered every question that the teacher had asked them and they were noisy. They spoke and whispered and made a lot of noise.

The teacher was nice to the students. She didn't yell at them all the time when they did something wrong. "Take out your books about the Vietnam war," she said. "Can anybody tell me what happen during the Vietnam Civil War?" A lot of people died," said one student. "What else happen?" said the teacher. "Many buildings were burned and people didn't have enough food to eat," said another student. She turned to the map and said, "the Vietnam war started here and it endend here."

She asked each student a question and they raised their hands. She walked around the classroom to make sure that each students are doing their work. Crrr Crrr Crrr, the telephone rang. "Hello?" the teacher said. "Blah, blah, blah, blah." The students got noisy. "sorry class, that was one of the parents on the phone." "Turn to your next page," the teacher said. She pointed to one of the students and told them to read. "Sit up!" she told one of the students. "How do you feel if someone talk about your country?" she asked one of the students. "I would feel sad."

She asked the students about how do they feel when a person is teasing them about their country and then she said "you kids learned a lot". "Very good."

She turned to us and said, "You guys have been patient, you can stay here or go next door. thanks for coming," she said. "By and nice to meet you!" we said. I kind of liked the class, because the teacher was nice and I liked the way she taught students.

attention. When the teacher absentmindedly tried to read a book that she had already read aloud before, her five-year-old audience protested loudly and gleefully. Anna's sense of decorum and her respect for teachers made it difficult for her to narrate this incident. I suggested she write down the conversation as she had heard it and see if that felt more comfortable. In the resulting account, the students are allowed their glorious moment of correcting the teacher, but the teacher is also portrayed as reasonable and understanding. When students and teachers spoke for themselves, Anna's discomfort disappeared:

> Then Ms. Perlet said, "Today I will read you a book about butterfly." All the students yelled, "You read us a book about butterfly already." Ms. Perlet said, "It's not the same book I read to you I got a different one." The students said, "Where is the book?" Ms. Perlet said, "Wait a minute let me find it. It is somewhere on my desk but I got big piles of papers and I can't find it right in this minute. Here it is." The students yelled again, "You read this book already." Ms. Perlet said, "I read a different one." "NO you read this one." The teacher started to read the book and show the pictures, the students yelled again. "You read this book already." Ms. Perlet, "Yes I did, I just realized that I read this book to you, but that's okay. I read it again to you. Sorry kids."

When students read this paragraph, they always enjoy hearing about the triumph of a successful challenge to the teacher, and teachers reading it inevitably think, "Oh yes, I've been *there* before."

The schedule I had planned at the outset proved to be overly ambitious. The small-group work, the peer editing, and the teacher conferencing all took longer than expected, but because it was such fruitful work, I had no desire to cut it short. The final activity in my original plan was an observation visit to the adult classrooms where the parents of many of my students were students themselves. But with the days slipping away, I substituted an interview in which students asked their parents to recall their own school days as English learners. To my surprise, the adult interview turned out to be one of the more meaningful pieces in the unit. Students wrote about the fears, embarrassments, and thrills that their mothers and fathers had experienced in school—feelings that were not unfamiliar to these middle-school students. Some related their parents' feelings of alienation:

> When my father didn't know any English he said that he felt like he is from another planet . . . He was scared when his teacher gave a paper to do because he was scared to make mistakes.
>
> *Anna Yakimiv*

> [My mother] said, "I felt like a deaf person and I felt lonely."
>
> *Ermias Ogbeab*

> When my aunt first didn't know English she felt lonely. She felt like she was the only human on this earth that didn't know English.
>
> *Fatuma Salongo*

Truc and her mother discussed some of the larger issues:

> My mom went to school at Westside Adult Learning Center for one year. When she was first learning English, she was very scared because she couldn't speak English. When she didn't know any English, she felt [it] was too difficult for her. She was worried about her life. She think how her life would be if she didn't know any English.
>
> *Truc Le*

My students saw and heard subtleties. They could distinguish between challenges and fears. After detailing all the problems her mother faced, Marina concluded proudly: "She was not scared at all, because she had never been scared of anything."

These adult learners brought my class back to the questions about being engaged learners. When they didn't understand what was going on in the class, they forged ahead with a variety of strategies. Anna's father "asked the Ukraine people that [had] been here longer." If she didn't understand, Marina's mother asked her teacher "to repeat what she said, and explain what does that mean." Truc's mother liked to look at books from the classroom library "when she have free time. She didn't know all the words but she still look at it." Now the parents were reinforcing what I worried had become my tired messages: learning strategies are very personal. The same ones don't work at the same time for everyone, and you must have the courage to do what works for you.

At the end of the interview, the students asked their parents, "What is the most important thing for an adult to do when he/she is trying to learn a new language?" They came back with loads of advice—words that I hoped would piggyback on some of the things they were beginning to recognize about themselves.

> My mother told me some important things for an adult to do when he or she is trying to learn another language. They would have to study new vocabulary words, never be shy, and always speak more.
>
> *Marina Konovalchuk*

> They have to [pay] attention, ask questions, don't be shy, and make friends.
>
> *Phitsamai Phonepasewth*

> The best things for an adult to do when he or she is trying to learn a new language is they have to talk to other people, and listen to people to hear how people pronounce the words . . . always ask question if they don't understand something.
>
> *Truc Le*

> If a person wants to learn English, he or she must go to the library and get easy books to help them learn English.
>
> *Fatuma Salongo*

> The most important thing . . . is Practice, Practice, Practice. It takes long time but just keep Practicing.
>
> *Anna Yakimiv*

Most of the adult interviews were conducted in the students' first languages. It was an opportunity for students to connect with their parents to discuss experiences and feelings they had in common. Like many busy families in America, my students' families were often struggling to keep up with the demands of jobs, parenting, and education (their children's and their own). The interview gave parents and students a chance to share the frustrations and triumphs of survival in a new school, in a new language. Many students wrote that this was the most meaningful part of the project for them.

> The project that I enjoy doing the most is interview my mom because it helped me understand my mom better. And also it fun to interview my mom and listen to [her] when she said some English words.
>
> *Truc Le*

> I really liked interviewing my mom. I found out that she is kind of like me.
>
> *Phitsamai Phonepasewth*

With the last day of classes looming before us, my teacher haranguing to complete the project was replaced by a wonderful student-centered motivation. A publishing event became our final exam in English. I invited the principal and other adults to visit for a conversation with the students about their work. As we prepared for that day, students sought each other out for help with corrections and rewrites. They asked to come in during lunch and after school. As for the grammar teaching that I had worried about at the beginning of the unit, much of it was being taught in the peer-editing conferences. The students wanted to get it right, because, as everyone now believed, these books *mattered*.

The immersion journalism project stretched the students' writing abilities in several ways. It helped them to move from first-person narration toward the more sophisticated personal essay genre. It showed them how a writer can approach a topic from different entry points, and how a group of essays can draw a more complex and multifaceted picture of a particular topic. It gave them a reason to attend to details and to create accurate and interesting dialogue. This project also challenged the students to use field trips and interviews for gathering information, and to observe and ask questions knowing that they would have to incorporate the information into an essay. It gave them a chance to create their own observation tools and interview questions based on what they considered germane to the topic of immigrant education.

Good immersion journalism pieces are really works of research. They have a teaching element, or "information transfer." In the immigrant-education project, this transfer works in two directions. Readers of these immigrant-education books will discover what it is like to struggle with a new educational system while learning a new language at the same time. In doing their research, my students also learned about the skills and strategies that hopefully will make their journey on to high school, college, and adulthood more successful.

My students and I also learned about one more crucial element of immersion journalism: risk taking. It wasn't something Lee focused on, and it certainly isn't unique to this kind of writing; nevertheless, it became a critical piece of my students' and my experience of immersion journalism. I really didn't want to go to Central Square to converse with strangers and look for a story. As it turned out, my anxiety was in direct proportion to the thrill of accomplishment when I managed to capture the experience on paper. It was a thrill I wanted my students to experience too, and so with the power that a teacher wields, I forced it on them. I was not so naive as to think that risk taking would be new to these students. They do it every day, each time they open their mouths or put pen to paper to communicate in a new language they have only imperfectly mastered. I only asked them to try a few new things, and the rewards—their pride in their accomplishments, their trust in their new-found writing skills—more than matched the risks I had asked them to take.

References

Bode, Janet. 1989. *New Kids on the Block: Oral Histories of Immigrant Teens.* New York: Watts, Franklin, Inc.

Reflections from a Colleague

Mary Fipp (Teacher, San Diego, California)

Upon reading Linda Reilly's narrative, I am struck immediately by the fact that she lives by one of the most important maxims of exemplary teaching: Don't ever ask your students to do what you yourself have not done. All too frequently, we give top-down instruction, never attempting to do the work we ask others to do. But how can an adult truly appreciate the efforts of a younger learner without having gone through the labor of the task? Without trying it oneself, there's no basis for comparison: no sensitivity to the effort, no empathy for or with the learner.

Linda's story is as much about facing fear and taking risks as it is about acquiring new skills in language learning. Linda is faced first with her own fear. Remember it was she who asked, "Wait . . . what if someone doesn't want to do this?" long before her students asked, "Do we have to *talk* to them? Will we be going into classes *alone*?" She knows how difficult this task is going to be for her students because she's been there. But it is precisely for that reason that she knows how far to push. "Yes, I'm asking a lot of you; I know how scared you feel, but trust me, it will be a rewarding learning experience."

Trust me . . . Each year, with every class, there's that precarious moment when students teeter on the edge of uncertainty, between trust and distrust. This hesitancy is even more pronounced with second-language students. So many are silent, waiting. "Am I safe? What will happen when I make a mistake? Will the other students laugh? Will the teacher get angry?" I gained a deeper appreciation for the emergent learner's reluctance to make the leap toward self-directed learning from reading the accounts of Fatuma's and

Ngoc's homeland school experiences. Ngoc reminds me how something as simple as a seating chart can shape a student's self-image. "The teachers are not fair to all the students if the parents of the students have a lot money or those who are smart kids they put those kids in the front [row] and those aren't get good grade they put them way back the end of the table." As Linda's students move toward trust, they begin to reveal more about themselves, using their writing as the vehicle.

Deciphering dialogue is one of the more difficult tasks when learning another language. Conversation proceeds so swiftly. "Was that a question or a statement? Did she say dressing? A salad dressing? A dressing room? A dress?" Even as a native English speaker, Linda had that very same experience at Woolworth's. When using immersion journalism, where so much depends upon dialogue, I wonder: what preliminary listening could precede the actual immersion? A pair of students might be given a situation, such as returning an item to a department store because it's too small. The students could play out that scenario while the immersion journalists (their classmates) practice taking down the conversation. Then the journalists could read aloud what they've recorded, performing it almost like a play. Does it sound like real speech? Were those the exact words? Even later, they could talk about how to capture accents and attitudes in written language.

Linda resists the temptation to give in to frustration. At the end of her well-planned lesson, the students "come up short" of her expectation. Still she moves forward, asking her students to discover how they can transform their "sluggish indirect quotations" into dialogue so vivid and rich that it *is* the essay. The patience and the tenacity of both teacher and students are rewarded with Fatuma's ingenious numbering system, the instrument she uses to rework her first "boring" rendition to produce a "better" piece of work.

Anna's vignette captures "Murphy's Law" beautifully. I can imagine that Mrs. Perlet, aware of her student visitors' needs, prepared a specific lesson that she was certain would provide the dialogue needed for a journalism project. But after several interruptions from her students, sure enough, it turns out she *has* read this book to her class before. What can she do? It fits the needs of the visitors;

there isn't time to make a last-minute switch, so she does what so many others have done in the same situation—she apologizes to her class and reads it again anyway. With keen insight, Anna has captured both the words and actions of this moment.

Perhaps without even knowing it, Marina Konovalchuk, Truc Le, and Phitsamai Phonepasewth share with us their respect for, and burgeoning intimacy with, their parents. It is those parents' faith in their children's futures that runs through the stories. That faith will create the "culture of possibility" of which Gándara speaks in *Over the Ivy Walls*. It is this connection through storytelling, common experience, and hope that will catapult these children into the world of possible achievement. It is this family link, the parental push for achievement, that tallies high among the reasons for immigrant success.

Linda Reilly's chapter is more than a recipe for immersion journalism in the second-language classroom. It is a series of little stories that underscore the value of hard work, as well as parental and public involvement, in the educational process. It validates Lucy McCormick Calkins words: "We write because we want to understand our lives" (1986, 3). No one, not even Mrs. Perlet, remains unchanged by the experience. Linda has set in motion what could become a whirlpool of achievement with teachers, students, and parents all gathered around it.

References

Calkins, Lucy McCormick. 1986. *The Art of Teaching Writing.* Portsmouth, NH: Heinemann.

Gándara, Patricia. 1995. *Over the Ivy Walls.* New York: State University of New York Press.

5

Are We There Yet?

Immersion Journalism as a Discussion of Good Work

Connie Russell-Rodriguez
with Javier Mendez, Marie Keem, and Dennie Palmer Wolf

With Excellence for All

American education is one long—and still continuing—effort to get equity and excellence to come together. In the century and a half that we have had public schools, we have tried out many tools to ensure that our commitment to education for all children doesn't translate into simply making a minimum amount of learning widely available. In the mid-1800s, we opened public elementary schools. At the close of the century, we opened growing numbers of public high schools. In the 1950s, the Supreme Court declared "separate but equal" education unfair. Since then we have tried busing, built magnet schools, and funded programs like Chapter 1 in an effort to see that all children receive a worthwhile education. We haven't won yet: poor and culturally diverse children continue to read, write, and do mathematics at levels far below their wealthier, safer, and more mainstream peers.

So the search for how to make a difference continues. Right now, we are trying to fashion still another tool—standards—in order to make public statements about what all students are entitled to learn. For example, at this moment, the National Council of Teachers of English and the International Reading Association are producing literacy standards; in Massachusetts a newly published set of curriculum frameworks alerts us to the various strands, including media, that compose contemporary literacy. Soon the city of Boston, where I teach, will release its own municipal expectations for students' reading and writing.

These standards are fine—as far as they go. As a long-time teacher of bilingual students, I am relieved to hear people making public statements about excellence that no longer exclude the children I teach. But I also know that no matter how articulate and equitable these standards are, there is a huge gap between announcing them and living by them. Frankly, writing and publishing the standards is child's play compared to the work of creating the economic and human conditions under which the standards are attainable. For example, from a teacher's perspective, one of the most difficult challenges of setting and holding to high standards for all students involves exchanging an "assignment culture" (where you just come to school, do the work, and take the grade) for an "excellence culture" (where you continue until the work meets or, even better, surpasses the standard). What is so hard about this? Only that it demands completely changing most familiar forms of classroom practice.

1. Quality has to be discussed, not left a well-kept secret.
2. Quality can no longer be based on doing the parts (having a cover sheet, a title, 350 words, an introduction, body, and conclusion). It has to be founded on fulfilling the dimensions of strong work (exhibiting a compelling question, vivid language, thoughtful use of diverse sources, etc.).
3. Work has to be continuously revisable.
4. There has to be ample support—models, discussions, tutoring—to enable even the most needy students to reach the standard.

The list may be short, but the task borders on monumental. Think about what is implied. First, teachers have to know and be able to articulate what is below, at, and beyond the standard. This demands a depth of knowledge no teacher's edition can supply. Classroom time has to be radically restructured to allow students to have continual re-entry to their work. It is essential to create carefully designed units that provide all students with the ingredients for excellence and to have concrete models of excellence—ideally from other students, as well as from adults. Teachers have to build a new repertoire of strategies for revision. If large numbers of students are going to hit the mark, revision can't be recopying in ballpoint and skipping lines. It has to become a set of strategies for substantial change. In other words, the question always before you and your class has to become "Are we there yet? Have we arrived at good work?"

Our Signature: Activism

My school, the Rafael Hernandez, is an ideal testing ground. It is a K–8 school near Egleston Square, in Boston. The Hernandez is a two-way bilingual school where students develop both English and Spanish as academic languages throughout the K–8 years. Every classroom contains both native English and Spanish speakers who come primarily from families with low incomes. Approximately 40 percent of students receive some form of special education. The middle school contains approximately eighty students from sixth through eighth grades. The school is situated in a neighborhood that many would call "tough," even "dangerous." However, in the last decade, the neighborhood has been turning the quality of life around, thanks to the hard work and dedication of a linked set of neighborhood agencies. One of the original schools involved in the Expeditionary Learning model of the New American Schools Development Corporation, the Hernandez has been working with a view of learning as a sustained journey into new territories of understanding. This work has also been an expedition—or several rolled into one—for teachers as much as for students. In this process, we have had to ask one another hard questions about what counts as quality. Thus, in all these respects, our students, families, community, and faculty all know what it is to fight towards quality, even against the odds.

As a result, our work has its own stamp or signature. Several expeditions, as well as much of the way we talk and teach, focused on the theme of activism, how individuals act on behalf of their peoples and communities to secure a better life. When we first introduce the topic of activism, students immediately think of monumental figures like Cesar Chavez or Malcolm X, but we also want them to study and appreciate the familiar individuals and organizations in their own community that refuse to let things be as they have always been. Therefore, while our expeditions are rooted in the history of well-known individuals and historical movements, we have long insisted that they include studies of living individuals who are active in neighborhood and city life. This springs from our belief that particularly in the challenging, even harsh, urban environments where our students become young adults, they cannot afford to grow up as victims or passive subjects. They—and their families—need an activist's energy, resilience, and generosity, especially now, when so much of what my students hear about immigrants and non–English speakers is selfish, even full of hatred.

The invitation to become part of the immersion journalism seminar provided the spark to bring these two strands—the concern for creating a culture of excellence and the urgent need for activism—together. We were in the middle of rethinking how to make the mandatory eighth-grade study of American history into a series of linked expeditions that were more than an excursion along the Freedom Trail or a visit to Plymouth Rock. So often my students are puzzled about why they should study "people back then." They want to know why history matters, especially when most of the materials available to us say little about the lives of people who were not English speakers, and not members of the mainstream culture. I saw in immersion journalism the first glimmers of how we could continue to emphasize the constructive role of activism, connect "then" and "now," and move our classroom conversations steadily toward the kind of excellent work that will make it possible for my students to belong, take part, and speak out.

Making a Difference

We designed an expedition, "Making a Difference," that was focused on Americans throughout history who have decided to take a stand on behalf of others. We knew we wanted to publish a magazine that would discuss what it takes to become an American brave enough to take a stand and to act on it, despite personal cost. Like all our expeditions, it had already had a long and evolving life. We originally taught it for the first time in the spring of 1995, following the immersion journalism seminar. We revised and retaught it again the following fall.

In both rounds, the first portion of this expedition found us deep in the history of the Americas. Working with materials from North, Central, and South America, our students studied the lives of people who elected to make a difference. In all cases, we worked across multiple sources of information—history textbooks, historical documents, historical fiction, and film—in order to build up a complex picture of both the conditions and the individual choices that lie behind an individual. The students began by reading a biography of Harriet Tubman by Ann Petry, which we chose specifically because it included a timeline that cross-referenced the events in Tubman's life with other simultaneous historical events. Thus, an individual heroine was placed in the context of earlier developments, specifically the wider effort to end slavery and the lives of other participants in that effort. The book also provided us with a first chance to urge excellence. We created a companion activity book/journal designed to prompt all students to think not only about the obvious aspects of reading comprehension, but also about the sources and significance of Harriet Tubman's life and actions as an activist. In this way, we tried to ensure that everyone had the basis for joining in class discussions. We were also trying to stress that a command of information and a hold on the details was vital. Students would never be strong journalists if they couldn't get the facts down. The result was that we had much more vigorous and searching conversations in class. Classroom discussion, even of topics as demanding as the role of singing in enslaved communities, began to have this kind of energy and detail:

STUDENT: It was the only thing they could do. It was like praying.
CONNIE: Did they sing "I hate my master, I want to be free!"?
STUDENT: They talked about following the river.
CONNIE: The word I'm going for is *symbolic*. There were a lot of references to Moses. What could Moses mean to them?

STUDENT: Someone was coming to take them out of bondage.
CONNIE: Harriet Tubman became known as Moses, even if people didn't know her real name . . . What about "follow the drinking gourd"?

As the discussion continues, students work out that "the drinking gourd" is a symbolic name for the Big Dipper, the constellation that escaping slaves could follow to freedom.

Before moving on to a new section, the students wrote their thoughts in the reflections section. This regularly occurring reflections page allowed students to respond in their own style and according to their own thoughts. Some drew pictures depicting scenes in Harriet Tubman's life, while others summarized the chapter and still others compared their own experiences with Harriet Tubman's or speculated about how they would react in her position. Here we were trying to guarantee that everyone had the chance to think about the large questions at stake, not just the definition of the term "abolitionist." For us, this kind of practice in discussing large questions was an absolutely necessary foundation for being able to take on the journalism assignment that would culminate the expedition.

In the next portion of the expedition, students acted together as a research community. Each one had to read and conduct research in order to produce two kinds of writing. The first was a review of a book or a film that they had used in their research. Students had the option of writing this review for either an English- or a Spanish-speaking audience. The point is that both languages have the power to communicate personal vision, large ideas, and reflections on history.

A Time for Justice

"A Time for Justice" is a video which informs people about what condition we were in, with the violence that had been occurring, during the years before the Civil Rights movement. The violence, destruction and taking of lives had happened many years ago. Yes these negative occurrences continue to happen (now) as the years ago.

This video is just a reminder of what are the changes that have happened since the civil rights movement began, and about the violence that has been happening during the past years.

Alexander Reyes

Harriet Tubman

Yo lei el libro *Harriet Tubman* por Ann Petry, una historia sobre una extraordinaria mujer llamada Harriet Tubman. La llamo extraordinaria por la vida que vivió. Ayudó a los esclavos librarse de la vida horrible que llevaban.

Harriet hizo 19 viajes hasta ar sur para ayudar a escapar a los esclavos. Todos sus viajes fueron largos, peligrosos, calurosos, y muy cansadores, pero ella no descansó hasta a tener su familia en libertad. Aunque era peligroso lo que ella hacia, no dejó que el miedo le paralizara. . . .

Miozoty Vega

[I read the book *Harriet Tubman* by Ann Petry, a history about an extraordinary woman named Harriet Tubman. I call her extraordinary because of the life she lived. She helped slaves free themselves from the horrible lives they had to bear.

Harriet made 19 trips to the south to help slaves escape. All her trips were long, dangerous, hot, and tiring, but she never rested until she delivered her family to freedom. Although what she did was dangerous, she never let her fear paralyze her.]

Students also wrote a short, summary biography of a person who had made a difference: Shirley Chisholm, Thurgood Marshall, Cesar Chavez, and others. Because Javier, my co-teacher, is a Colombian with vivid memories of participating in one of the many student revolutions of the 1960s and 1970s, we were able to bring a deliberately pan-American perspective to our historical work. Students studied and wrote about figures like Luis Muñoz Marin and Rigoberta Menchu right alongside Marshall and Chavez.

In many cases we were pleased—for a beginning. Students appeared to be getting several important ideas. The first was that their biographies moved, at least a few steps, away from paragraphs copied straight out of the encyclopedia. Students understood, to some degree, that they were meant to be explaining the conditions of their subject's life, selecting the high points, and evaluating the key choices that person had made. Also, we began to see the first hints of writing that didn't plod—words and phrases that caught some of the fire of those brave individual choices. When they were finally assembled, these pieces gave us the section of our publication "Activists in History."

With this as background we were ready to move toward our immersions in the lives of current activists. But not without first building the tools students needed. An important part of immersion journalism is becoming aware of intimate details that help paint the scene, and that turn the writer into someone who has an inside perspective to relate to the reader. This means being very observant. To get into this idea, we had someone observe our class and type up notes for the kids to look at. They thought she was incredibly nosy, but we pointed out that she had gotten down a lot of good details. Here are her notes:

> Activity: Watching video about the Civil Rights Movement Situation: Lights are out, the shades are down, everyone is quiet and watching the video. There is not much other movement. General observations:
>
> - There are 20 students in the room.
> - The bulletin board across from me has a purple background.
>
> The only thing on the board is a sheet of paper from a large pad which says:
> Rubric for Descriptive Writing
>
> **1.** Use descriptive adjectives.
> **2.** Include details.
> **3.** Use verbs that show action.
>
> - To the left of the sheet with writing on it hangs the whole pad of blank sheets.
> - J. is turned to the window. Another boy is also turned to the window.

- F. is writing something. There is violence on the screen and she looks up then looks back to her paper. At the same time a couple of the boys exchange words.
- S. is looking in her notebook and flipping through the pages. She doesn't look up.
- A couple of other girls are working on other papers.
- Connie is standing directly across from the TV, leaning against the heater, with her eyes looking straight at the screen.
- Two girls in front of me are having a quiet conversation.

Shortly after that we started our own observations. Students went in pairs to another classroom at the Hernandez, where they observed for fifteen minutes, then they came back with their observations and talked about everything that they had written down. The follow-up was to write their observations in a story format, for which we talked about using descriptors and interesting verbs to tell the story of what they saw. In order to provide a model and a basis for discussion of how the transition from notes to a story occurs, I took the earlier notes from the outside observer and wrote a story based on them:

> **Write-up**
> "Rubrics for Descriptive Writing" is what meets my eye as I walk in. It is a fairly spacious room with the desks arranged in pairs and about 20 students of various shades. They are watching a movie, and some of them are interested, yet some seem less so. Is it that the movie isn't interesting, or do they have their minds filled with other, more pressing problems?
>
> The teacher is in the back of the room, eyes on the television and apparently engrossed in the movie. Beside her a distracted boy turns toward the window. The shade is down . . . what could he be looking at?

We then listened to an interview called "A Boy's Shelter for Street People" from a taped National Public Radio program. We wanted the students to think about asking good questions, but the content was too absorbing to pick apart for technique.

Even so, students were able to hear how the interviewer's open-ended questions pushed the interaction along and made the story more complex. Building on this, we set up a mock interview and asked two students to take on the role of the interviewer; one was to be an attentive person interested in getting at the interviewee's story, the other was to be a poor interviewer. It worked remarkably well. What emerged is that although our students had had a difficult time listing the qualities of a strong and poor interview, they *could* get these qualities into their performances. For instance, the poor interviewer was distracted, playing with his pencil, and staring off into space. The observing students immediately picked up on what they admired in the good interviewer and generated a list of characteristics that we used throughout the remaining portions of our journalism expedition:

A Good Interviewer
maintains eye contact
talks clearly
is observant
is friendly
shows interest
is curious
is flexible
asks good questions
looks for stories

We drove these points home when we invited Mel King, a well-known and very active local figure, to speak to us. Ahead of time, we brainstormed questions based on the fact that Mel King was active in politics in Boston and that he had run for mayor. King is a very quietly charismatic person, he doesn't walk into the room and blow you away. Yet, in part because of their new interest in being interviewers, they all listened closely as he spoke for about forty-five minutes about his history as a Boston-based activist. The students did the interview at the very end. We videotaped the interview and that let us review what happened. When we watched it with the cool eyes of observers and critics, many students heard King preface several of his answers with phrases such as "Like I said before . . ." Instantly, they recognized that he was signaling that he thought he had already given this information. In those few minutes, virtually every eighth grader learned about the importance of using a list of questions flexibly. This is evident even in a short sample of the classroom dialogue that followed:

CONNIE: Okay, so what does it mean to be flexible [in your questioning]?
STUDENT: You have other questions.
CONNIE: Is going through your list and asking every question being flexible? When might you not want to ask a question?
STUDENT VOICES: When a speaker has already covered it.

We also went after what *exactly* they meant when they said that an interviewer asks good questions. As we talked I worked with the list of criteria on the board.

CONNIE: So what is a good question?
STUDENT: They make sense and have to do with what you know.
STUDENT: They are open-ended.
CONNIE: What is open-ended?
STUDENT: It takes more than one word to answer.
CONNIE: Give me an example.
STUDENT: Why do you like . . .
CONNIE: Or, "Tell me a story from when . . ." Stories are what help you know people.

Having done this careful work with tools, we were as ready as we could be for the next phases in our expedition. In the first excursion, students went on a scavenger hunt that took them throughout Boston. They had to put their observation skills to work: finding locations, monuments, plaques—even a restaurant in Chinatown where they could eat as inexpensively as possible. The expedition included working in a soup kitchen serving dinner. As with any expedition, this one contained not only the inevitable organizational frustrations, but totally unforeseen events that taught in ways it would have been impossible to plan. In this case it was an unexpected interview in which students learned about getting beneath the surface of expectations and stereotypes. A student's account portrays this clearly:

Food Not Bombs

When we got to Food Not Bombs, we were greeted with lots of smiling faces from other volunteers. Food Not Bombs is a completely volunteer organization that makes food and serves it to the homeless . . . Before we got there we all went thinking that the homeless were living in the streets because they did something wrong. I went expecting to feed the homeless. I never expected to get to know them and become their friend.

Some of the people were living on the streets because of reasons like they had just left an abusive relationship and they had nowhere to go and no one to turn to, or other things such as they lost their jobs and had no way to pay mortgage or rent, or they got into an argument with their spouse and their spouse kicked them out of the house.

As I finished serving one homeless woman, an older guy with short blond and gray streaked hair, who was also homeless, walked up to me and put a crooked smile on his face. I dropped my hands down to my sides and looked straight into his dead, bluish green cat eyes. I froze for a moment; my eyes seemed to be turning a dark devil's red as tears slowly began rolling down my face.

He took a clean napkin, wiped my tears and tried to comfort me. He told me that it was okay to cry and he had tears, too. His eyes started to bulge, I could see his veins in his head, and tears began to run down his cheeks as he told me how he became homeless. He was a veteran in the army. When he got back to America after Vietnam he had no home, no family, nowhere to go and no money. He had no choice but to go to a shelter or live on the streets . . .

This trip has changed my thoughts about the homeless and helping my community more. I hope that this article has changed your thoughts about the homeless and has encouraged you to help your community. I hope you know what you have is luxurious compared to some of the things that other people have and that you should appreciate it.

Ebony Williams

Immersion Experiences

After our urban exploration, it was time for the students to go out individually and to step into the lives of local activists, spending a day at work shadowing them. We had spent hours ahead of time talking with our former colleagues and contacting people they thought might be interested. Finally, we had a list of people at community health services, educational centers, and other organizations.

Going to places, asking questions, and interviewing turned out to have been a very effective dress rehearsal for our students. Even though they were anxious when they went out to spend a full day with an individual, they were brave and competent—most kids came back with as many as six pages of notes. They all had different experiences, but no one was disappointed. Except perhaps the teachers. Those half-dozen pages of notes the students returned with were full of the facts—but that is all. The bare bones were present—but little insight, no sense of character, and few of the stories we had talked so long and hard about.

We were lucky, however. We had scheduled students to visit someone for one day and then return for a follow-up day a week later. This was really good foresight. It was obvious when we talked after the first day that the whole process of shadowing, interviewing, and creating a profile of an unusual individual wasn't at all clear to students. Also, students didn't get anywhere near the information they needed to be able to write it up the way we wanted. We revisited an immersion piece that another PACE teacher had written on his journey into Central Square, Cambridge. It was a remarkable portrait of a young woman whose life had, for a time, gone bottom up. By combining acute visual observation (he had even sketched a portrait) along with information and direct quotations from his conversations with her, Clyde had created a complex and sympathetic glimpse into the life of someone fighting back from difficulty. This time we went through his piece with a fine-tooth comb picking out the different pieces of information, surmising how Clyde had gotten them, and looking at how he introduced them into the flow of his piece (Figure 5–1).

FIGURE 5–1. *Clyde Yoshida's Immersion Piece with Comments*

She doesn't bother to get close to people in the shelter anymore. She's afraid of losing these relationships. America's promise let her down. She said she panicked when her parents divorced. She put her money into her education, never finished school and lost all of her money. Admitting to not being 100% right now, there was still some talk of owning a house and getting her son back. That little notch in her forehead became slightly more pronounced as she spoke of this. Social workers considered her to be unfit to raise her baby. The father's parents have him down in Florida. Paul is three and a half years old.

shows worry

"Paul has the best of his father and mother," she confided. She also wanted me to know that she doesn't want them to make any preconceived plans for him.

She spread her left hand and lightly pinched her gold band between her thumb and index finger.

Shows her touching the ring when she talks about it.

"This isn't a wedding ring. It represents the love for my son, hardship and poverty. I think if you are rich you need to be generous," she said.

Maybe she needs to know it's real?

I asked her again about the ring's symbolism.

"I don't want people to think I endured all this without the institution of marriage. I wear the ring to prove them wrong."

Excerpt from Clyde Yoshida's Immersion Journalism piece
PACE Curriculum Seminars, December 1994

We also went through an article about Tom Cruise that had appeared in *Life Magazine*. Every time something was communicated we asked, "OK, now which is that, observation or information?" and said, "OK, that piece of information the interviewer had to have asked because there's no way that the interviewer would know that unless they'd asked a question." Then there were other things: how he was dressed, how far down his shirt was unzipped, that kind of stuff. Obviously you don't have to ask somebody, "Excuse me, can I measure that?" That's observation. As we did that, we talked about "This is how we want your write-ups to be, a combination. We want you to mix observation, the interview questions, and quotes so that you get a real feel for the person." And we talked a little bit with the students about style. We pointed out that in the Tom Cruise article everything was short. All the sentences were short and choppy and everything went by fast, and in a couple of places the author actually says, "He's a very fast character." So we all talked about the congruency between style and the personality the author was describing. As we ended the discussion of the Tom Cruise article, a couple of kids said, "Well, I don't know that information about my person!" and our reply was, "Well, that's why you're going back on Wednesday!" Until they had focused access to concrete examples of how other writers pieced together their portraits, students simply thought their assignment was to write up a description of the person's *job*, not of the person as someone whose history and experiences drew them into making change in the community. With this new understanding in mind, we created a web of questions for the second round of interviewing and observation. These questions were hugely different from the simple name, age, salary inquiries that students had begun with. Now students wanted to know about the person's childhood, their life as a young adult, and what drew them to activism. The results appeared in the section of our final publication entitled "The Faces of Activism in Boston." In the end, these portraits let us see the clothes, the offices, and the hearts and minds of a wide cross-section of the people working in health care, teen programs, and shelters. Looking over these interviews as a teacher, I am proudest of the fact that you can really see the results of students having learned to interview: to ask questions, to listen to the answers, to pick out critical quotes, and to reflect on what they have heard. An excerpt from Edson Jean's interview of Darren Clark shows this quality of give and take:

> Darren Clark decided to work in Dimock because he wanted to work with young people in the community. It's important for young people in the community to see a positive black man doing something productive that benefits them.
>
> Darren has been working at Dimock for three years. In fact, this year is going to be his fourth. . . . He used to work in the Department of Youth Services (DYS) and from there he worked at an alternative school where he was the chief executive officer (CEO).
>
> In Darren's opinion, the government is not building schools any more, they are building jails. Many kids are going to jail at early ages, and cops don't dress like cops; most of them are undercover. That's why it's important for us young kids to get a productive education to become successful adults. He thinks that we don't have to go to college to be a successful person, but I told him that I, Edson Jean, am looking forward to going to college. "You are a very well-thought young man," he said to me, "because having knowledge is the basis of surviving."

The writing mattered, no question. But it is also true that there were personal effects that went way beyond literacy. Reflecting on these effects, it is clear that the students who were influenced were the ones who had the strongest role models or who were really well matched with their mentors. For example, one student spent the field days with a young man who does outreach to kids in gangs. He left a deep imprint on the student especially because as a younger man he had been out on the streets and not doing wise things. His honesty was stunning. As a teacher, I was very affected to read what my students wrote about taking for granted their own circumstances. Considering that we look at these kids as "at risk, underprivileged," whatever, to have them saying "Wow, I'm so lucky I have all these things" was really eye-opening.

Reflections: Our Own and Theirs

Finally, students wrote a personal reflection that looked back either on their immersion experience or on the expedition as a whole. In our publication, these reflections took the form of letters to the editor, which seemed much more in line with our commitment to activism. In many respects, for our students, these kinds of public writing will be critical for the well-being of their communities. But, in looking over these reflections, what you see is how often an intensely personal experience turns out to be the key to understanding what lies at the heart of activism. Madelyn Aponte's piece, remembering back to her meetings with homeless people, makes this clear:

> One thing that I was really grateful for was serving breakfast to the homeless at the Boston Common. Yes, I know that I cried a lot, and people might think it was stupid, but it was that I first got butterflies and then I had a feeling that I never got before inside my heart. I was proud that I did what I did for the homeless. But I just can't understand why some people couldn't get it in their heads that what I felt was a feeling I never had before.
>
> One thing I realized was that, yes, at first it was stupid, but if you understood the feeling that I had inside my heart you'd know that it was just too painful to understand it or explain it. . . .
>
> One of the men came to talk to Ebony and me, telling us that crying was okay, that crying wasn't against the law and if you want to cry just to get your tears or feelings out it was okay. He also told us that crying was something natural and there was nothing wrong with crying. When this nice man told this to Ebony and me, I felt pretty good because this small talk put a smile on my face and because I felt like someone understood why and how I felt.
>
> *Madelyn Aponte*

When we do this expedition again, it will change just as radically as it did in the first revision. If we want writing that takes your heart out or drives home a point, then it cannot happen in eight weeks. That was only enough time for students who were already good writers. But the students who were still playing catch-up never had the chance to get past writing dry, detailed narratives. So are we there yet? No. But like the activists we studied, we are determined to make a difference

References

Petry, Ann. 1955. Harriet Tubman. New York: HarperCollins Publishers.

Reflections from a Colleague

by Kathy Greeley (Teacher, Cambridge, Massachusetts)

The issue of high standards matters to me; in fact, it has been on my mind a lot lately, ever since Dr. John Silber, the new chairman of the Massachusetts Board of Education, declared the idea that all children can learn at high levels "rubbish." I would like to send him Connie's article. There he would have to face how it is possible for strong teachers like Javier and Connie to "create a culture of excellence" while exploring issues of both interest and relevance to their students' lives.

The truth is that Connie and Javier support my view of what it is to *prepare* students to do good work. I love how Connie and Javier carefully broke down the skills they wanted to teach and provided authentic models of each practice. So often, we ask students to do something without giving them the skills or tools they need to be successful doing it. Of course, a few kids magically "get it" and produce one or two models of excellence. We wonder why other children aren't as quick or gifted. If we want a "culture of excellence" where everyone is held to high standards, we must provide students with the stepping stones to reach that goal.

For example, how many times do teachers ask children to do an interview with no preparation? Sometimes we feel we have "prepared" our students because we spent one class period practicing with each other. But not Connie and Javier. They know to begin by bringing an observer into the classroom. Students, especially at that age, are very interested in themselves. Of course, an outsider's observations of their world would be of great interest. But for Connie and Javier the work did not stop there. Then they had students observe other classrooms; analyze a narrative about their own classroom before writing their own observations; analyze professional interviews; develop their own list of criteria for good interviews by practicing it with each other; and critique their own interviewing skills using video. Only *then* did the students go out into the field. Even then, students were not fully ready to be astute interviewers with their community activists. Connie frankly expresses disappointment with the first round of interviews her students conducted. But she turns this "failure" into another stepping stone to excellence. Her description of the first round of interviews as a "dress rehearsal" is a wonderful reminder to us all to build opportunities for students to practice, rehearse, analyze, and revise. The important message is that the teachers did not accept the work as it was, nor did they just give up and decide "these kids" just can't do high-quality work. They looked at what was missing in their students' understanding of the project and figured out a way to help them reach the standard.

I also enjoyed how rooted in the community this expedition, "The Faces of Activism in Boston," was. When I look at the student piece on homelessness, I am struck by its vividness. The writer doesn't pull away into safe or rosy generalities—she can stay close to her encounter and to her own feelings:

> As I finished serving one homeless woman, an older guy with short blond and gray streaked hair, who was also homeless, walked up to me and put a crooked smile on his face. I dropped my hands down to my sides and looked straight into his dead, bluish green cat eyes. I froze for a moment; my eyes seemed to be turning a dark devil's red as tears slowly began rolling down my face.

Working at Food Not Bombs clearly brought alive the issues of hunger and homelessness for this student in a way no amount of lectures, class discussions, reading, or book-based research ever could. I frequently tell students to "show, don't tell" in their writing. "Let your characters speak for themselves," I say. "Don't tell me about the place, show it to me." Rather than *tell* her students about homelessness, Connie *showed* them. This experience gave a human face to issues that can feel very distant for many of us, and challenged the student to examine her own stereotypes and assumptions. Furthermore, by participating in a project that she could see helped other people, she learned an important lesson about activism. Too often, people feel hopeless or cynical about making a difference in their community. By giving her student an opportunity to engage in the real world, Connie showed her that she can touch other people's lives.

I very much appreciate the honesty of Connie's closing lines: "Are we there yet? No. But like the activists we studied, we are determined to make a difference." The realities of teaching, especially in urban public schools, can often be discouraging. While we need to keep our standards and expectations high, we also need to be patient and committed to the process of bringing all students along on the road to excellence.

6

All Across San Francisco

Immersion Journalism Through Photography and Video

Kamara Juarez

My school, Ben Franklin Middle School, sits in the heart of what native San Franciscans call the Fillmore district. As a neighborhood, it predates the fire and the earthquake; some of its Victorian structures even survived the destruction that nearly leveled the city. But in the century that followed, the neighborhood underwent immense changes, especially after World War II. Its Japanese families were dislocated by internment, and many of its resident African-American workers, drawn to the city by wartime industry, were abruptly unemployed at the war's end. (It is their descendants, many of whom continue to struggle to find jobs, who still live in the neighborhood.) Many of the historical buildings have disappeared. So it came as no surprise that when I proposed a journalism project that included a walking tour of the Fillmore, the grandmother of one of my students came to school disturbed and concerned. "What's there to see?" she asked sternly. "There's nothing there." Quickly, I pulled out a book on the history of the district, full of old maps and photographs. Looking down at the map of the Fillmore of days gone by, she studied it carefully and then pointed to a jewelry store where, she said, remembering, "I bought my first diamond." She remembered the candy store and the gas-lit street lamps. Suddenly it all made sense to her: there *were* things there. In many ways, the story of immersion journalism at Ben Franklin is contained in that exchange. Like this concerned grandmother, we encountered irresistible visual experiences that unleashed curiosity, understanding, and new possibilities.

I came back from the journalism seminar at PACE excited—but uncertain. The colorful and checkered past of the Fillmore is reflected in the mixture of students who come to Ben Franklin. They bring with them knowledge and languages from their cultures, as well as the histories of their families and neighborhoods: Chinatown, the Spanish-speaking Mission district, the Tenderloin (which is exactly what you might expect), as well as the Fillmore. The cultural diversity of the classroom brings with it a range of learning styles. Some students never speak at all in class, but write volumes. Others jump out of their seats and call out answers when they have something to add—but hate the stillness and isolation that goes with writing. Their literacy levels are at least as varied. Some read and write well above their grade level, while others struggle with elementary decoding skills. Boys and girls, becoming young men and women, sometimes teased and sometimes shunned one another. How could they, as a class, become journalists? How could I, as their teacher, insist that each and every one of them observe, interview, write, and edit?

One evening, while I was still turning over these questions, I met an old friend, Jim Crowley, a photographer whose work I admired. He wanted to work with students. Something germinated. Couldn't journalism be visual? Wasn't it possible that my students—who dashed off pieces and groaned at editing—could be engaged in creating a *visual* exploration? As Jim and I talked, I remembered how many of my students wanted to be in a project group when we studied clothing and how they had insisted on dressing a live model. When we studied Gilgamesh, they were fascinated by a photo of the Standard of Ur, a carving depicting war on one side, and on the other, peace. They had quickly picked out the king as the largest figure. Coming back to the conversation, I heard myself talking about immersion journalism, my students, and my sudden excitement about possibly using photography. Jim leapt in and began explaining about a film he had made from still photographs. In a matter of minutes, we had outlined a project about exploring the neighborhoods of the city. It would take us four months, much trial and error, and huge effort. It would also give my students a remarkable kind of visual literacy—as full of choice, style, collaboration, discussion, investigation, and editing as any piece of writing ever was.

Several weeks later, Jim arrived bringing the materials to make simple pinhole cameras. We went outside and learned how to use them to capture an image. The next day he was back and the air in my classroom filled with terms like *focus*, *contrast*, *f-stops*, and *exposure*. Students each stepped up to a real camera mounted on a tripod to take one carefully chosen shot. One of them, Darnell, broke step. He asked, "Do we have to take it from here?" With that, he turned the camera 180 degrees away from the park and out to the skyline of the city. The very next day Jim brought the slides of the kids' work from the park. As the images filled the screen, he talked with them about contrast, composition, and exposure. In that way, he began to give them standards for thinking about their images as more than casual snapshots. One after another the images flashed up on the screen—one frame of funny faces and goofy poses after the next. Then, unexpectedly, Darnell's image of St. Mary's cathedral seen in the distance filled the screen. The room was suddenly quiet as Jim praised how the photographer had framed the building and produced a startling image. It was my first inkling of what this work with visual language would make possible. Since the beginning of the year, Darnell had been almost antisocial, never doing his work, constantly negative. Even in the weeks of planning our photography trips to the neighborhoods, he had been loud and disruptive. But there he was: an intuitively talented visual author, willing to take chances, ready to work.

Becoming a Company of Visual Journalists

For our first full-fledged immersion, I had planned a visit to Golden Gate Park, where a herd of bison graced an open field. I dusted off my unit on the buffalo, and taught my students about the buffalo's significance to Native Americans as evidenced through the hunt, mythology, and the hundreds of uses they made of the animal. I imagined my students primed to make images that would reflect all this power and mystery. Who could have foretold an unstoppable rain that closed the park for weeks?

Luckily, San Francisco is a city full of possibilities. We had just finished reading *Sadako and the Thousand Paper Cranes*. My class was extremely curious about World War II and its effects on the city. As a culminating project, they had designed a statue to honor Sadako. So we piled onto a city bus—students; Jim; our resource specialist, Marilyn Tousey; and me—and headed for the Japanese Tea Garden, an entire world of plants, goldfish, ponds, bridges, and tea house built around the turn of the century. Partway there, a disoriented older woman at the back of the bus began to scold and, eventually, to curse me. Suddenly, what had been a noisy collection of loud adolescents coalesced into a tightly knit group. They spoke back to the woman, firmly saying, "You can't talk to our teacher like that." Thus began *our* journey, which my students would later title "All Across San Francisco."

Only fifteen students could enter the garden at once. While Jim and Marilyn took the boys, the girls and I climbed up onto the open stage of the band shell. I wanted them to develop the art of observing, rather than always zooming past things. So there, overlooking the maple trees, we sat and I taught them about how the brief syllables of Japanese haiku could capture a sudden, brief perception. I wanted them to think about those kinds of images in contrast to those of the bombings of Hiroshima and Nagasaki and the portraits of children in internment camps, playing behind barbed wire. I imagined them reflecting on Sadako's courage. I anticipated their comparing the images of war and the serenity of the garden. I could almost hear the journal entries they would write—descriptive and thoughtful.

My students did become engrossed in their surroundings. But it had nothing to do with the lessons I had taught. They played. Instead of bickering or clustering in their usual small groups, students moved through the landscape together, observing, wholly engaged in a shared visual experience. As one of my students wrote:

> The gate to the Japanese Tea Garden welcomed us as it had welcomed millions of guests in the past. The sight of the cherry blossoms made us forget the rainy weather that kept us locked up for almost three straight months. The fresh air and the bright sunlight made us feel happy and free . . . We were happy to be together in this peaceful place, away from school. We were enjoying this time out in the open, and we were getting to know each other in different ways.
>
> *Ben Pon*

The day in the Tea Garden erased many of the barriers that had existed in the class. It was amazing how much of the negative interaction disappeared once we left the classroom. The students reflected on this in their journals. They formed a notion of "us." And they wrote about working hard to continue the privilege of exploring outside the school walls. When their photographs came back, they sealed our commitment. We were now a group with a purpose, and, collectively, we possessed the tools to achieve success.

The Beginnings of Research

Any piece of journalism requires research, whether it takes the form of reading up on your history, looking at old photographs, finding the right people to interview, or asking questions that turn up intriguing answers. But my students thought of research only as copying paragraphs from the encyclopedia onto lined paper. I knew we would have to change that—shake it up, in fact.

As I mentioned earlier, Ben Franklin sits in the middle of the Fillmore District, a neighborhood of the city that has a full and complex history. Many old Victorian buildings are gone, along with the famous testament to the 1960s, the Fillmore Auditorium—both victims of the mistakes of urban renewal. My students come to Ben every day, but some have never even walked around the block. I thought that if I could show my students all the history hidden in buildings they thought of as hardly worth noticing, I might be able to give them a sense of what research was really all about. And from the moment Tamaya's grandmother was drawn into the map of her neighborhood as it used to be, I knew I was right. Not only did she give Tamaya permission to explore the district, she filled her granddaughter with all the stories she could remember. It was our first encounter with genuine research. Where once there had been a stern grandmother, there came to be a living library of history and wisdom about the neighborhood.

> My grandma told me all about the Fillmore District, how it used to be when she was a little girl like me. The Fillmore District has changed a lot over the years. This check-cashing place used to be a skating rink. It must have been fun to go skating with your friends . . . Where have all the good times gone? The Fillmore District has nothing to offer to our generation.
>
> *Tamaya Wellington*

Hearing about the Fillmore and its history helped students to begin to see beneath appearances. It was contagious. When students began to interview people in the neighborhood, they got a sudden sense of their own growing knowledge:

> This place is going out of business; so did the produce market right next to it. Almost the whole block is going out of business . . . We went into almost every store. A lot of them didn't know about the places that had been there before them.
>
> *Tiffani Johnson*

Some students even began to make connections to their study of ancient civilizations:

> The Fillmore is just like the world. It changes from old to new to old to new. See how the old church steeples stand out against the fresh paint of the apartment building?
>
> *Mical Asefaw*

As we prepared for another exploration, this time to Chinatown, I was excited to carry our research farther afield. Students read an excerpt from Amy Tan's *The Joy Luck Club* in which she describes her memories of the displays in the windows, the smells of a nearby bakery, and the image of a worn slide at the Chinatown playground. In the midst of these preparations, a Chinese-American student, William, came to me. Apprehensively, he asked, "Miss Juarez, why are we going to Chinatown? Kids are gonna make fun of our language and all the different foods in the windows. It will be embarrassing." I cringed. Would all our progress toward becoming one working group crumble? Was he right? Would the students laugh and make fun?

The innate curiosity and wonder of eleven- and twelve-year-olds prevailed. They searched out all that Tan had promised: Waverly Place where Tan grew up, the bakery, and the fish and ducks in the grocery windows. Students scoured the crowded streets, using their cameras to collect new sights and impressions. Rather than their earlier snapshots, students began to take photographs: images that drew a viewer's eyes to what had been discovered (Figure 6–1).

In fact, students were hungry to know more than looking alone could tell. But the language barrier stopped them. Even the street signs were in Chinese. For example, one student wanted to know why many of the roofs curved up at the ends. He grabbed William by the arm, pointed to a local man who looked wise with age, and begged William to ask the man his question. William turned to the old man and spoke in fluent Mandarin. The answer came back and William translated it smoothly. The upturned eaves prevented evil spirits from entering the building because they would slide off the roof. In that moment, William went from being a boy embarrassed about his own culture to becoming an informed guide, able to acquire and share new information as he moved between two languages and connected two cultures.

From Fact to Feeling

Our trip to Ocean Beach took us to a long stretch of sand along the Pacific that had once been the site for day outings and amusements for city residents. I had provided the students with a visual history of the area using books picturing what the area had at one time

FIGURE 6–1. *Curved-roof Building in Chinatown*

been. They had seen the turn-of-the-century splendor of the Sutro Baths and the famous Cliffhouse. When we actually stood on the site, my students were startled by what they saw: violent wind beating on the ocean, graffiti warning "Your children will pay," and deserted shells of the once-splendid buildings:

> Down below the Cliffhouse on a bedrock is the remains of the Sutro Baths. Sutro Baths was San Francisco's public bath in the 1800s and early 1900s . . . Now you can climb down the hill and walk through the ruins. The skeletons of the pool

show through the water and it is spooky. Some of the kids in our class say it's haunted, and that they'll never go back. Is it a coincidence that there have been so many fires and shipwrecks here at Seal Rock? You be the judge.

Jennifer Brackett

We hiked down to the cave where the salt water enters the bath area. Some of the students were scared. On our way home in the bus we laughed about it. But as I listened to our talk, I realized that my students were ready to do more than report and collect facts. They had become keen observers picking up hints and clues. They were now ready to use their observations creatively. The next day, I challenged them to use what they had learned from history together with what they witnessed themselves to write a story, "The Class Nightmare." The results were an astounding combination of observation and invention:

It all started one nice, sunny day. We thought this was another one of those normal field trips, but this one was deadlier.

We all came to Miss Juarez's room, we ate our lunch in the classroom, then we left. We thought it was going to be cool, but when we got there it wasn't so cool after all. It was very windy. It felt as if we were flying. Then Andrew said something weird, "The wind is warning us." I just stared back, and we walked down the hill.

We all saw where the Sutro Baths used to be. It looked haunted, especially the cave. Suddenly, the wind picked up, throwing sand in our faces. It really hurt. That's when I heard someone say, "Get out while you still can."

Marvin Peraza-Rivera

An Emerging Theme

Strong journalism is more than a collection of scenes. The entire piece must circle around an idea or a point, each one making the whole deeper with detail and reflection. But much of my students' experience has been shaped by daily assignments: "Here do this, for tomorrow, because it is what comes next in the book." Connections across assignments are few. So are "big pictures" and themes. Synthesis is rare. As recently as our trip to the Tea Garden, I was convinced that I had to tell students what to look for and how to make sense of what they found. But our repeated field trips and conversations had begun to change that. By the time we traveled to Ocean Beach, the students were on the edge of bringing their experiences together around a single large and pressing question.

As a part of our expedition to Ocean Beach, my students had also learned about Playland, a huge amusement park, complete with fun house, rickety roller coaster, booths for hot dogs and cotton candy. Many of them had interviewed their parents about outings and adventures at Playland. These exchanges brought the carnival atmosphere of the now-razed buildings back to life. Students hungrily questioned Marilyn Tousey, who could still remember bumper cars and the Ferris wheel. They imagined what fun it would be if Playland still were there. They drew pictures of the famous roller coaster and infamous Laughing Sal, a lady clown statue that stood in front of Playland, laughing constantly.

But when we arrived, we were greeted by overpowering winds hurling sand in our faces. As we trudged along the beach to meet Jim Crowley at an empty lot where Playland once stood, we moved through a devastating landscape of condominiums and parking lots. Students wanted to know what had happened. That night they reinterviewed their parents and found out about the vandalism, fires, and drug dealing that had led the city to tear down Playland:

> There used to be an amusement park right across the street. It was before our time, but we've seen pictures and heard stories. Playland was a great amusement park with a big slide, Ferris wheel, and giant, rickety roller coaster. Laughing Sal welcomed children to the Fun House. Unfortunately, times changed and people brought drugs, violence and destruction to Playland. It closed in the early seventies. Now you have to pay fifty cents to make Sal laugh, but she doesn't look as happy.
>
> *Narration from class video "All Across San Francisco"*

These observations connected to what students had learned in the Fillmore about the disappearance of ice cream stores, movie houses, and the skating rink. As we rode back on the bus, and in class later, students began to ask what had happened to recreation for young people over the past few decades. They wondered why newspapers and magazines can picture young people their age as "bad seed"—dangerous and without direction—and never mention how cities like San Francisco have stopped offering opportunities for safe recreation. Unfortunately, this insight emerged close to the end of the school year, when the pressure was on to produce our final video. Consequently, we never had the chance to reorganize our documentary around this question. Nonetheless, it was important that it emerged at all. My students had, perhaps for the first time, observed, gathered visual evidence, interviewed, and thought their own way into research. At last, they were circling around a question that could organize their work.

Choice and Revision

My students were no strangers to revision. I talked about it and requested it on most of their major assignments. But, for many of them, the regular answer was, "I did it once. I'm not gonna change it." Others simply recopied in ball-point pen. A few added adjectives or details. So when our field trips and first draft notes were over, and it was time to create a final film, I was frankly worried. Would students persist without the carrot of outings? Would they go back to bickering? Would they toss off first drafts and call it a day?

I began to be reassured when Jim and I took one of our students, Davinia, to the Main Library to help us select historical photographs to include in the film. This particular student was, to my knowledge, a slow reader who found writing challenging. Earlier research assignments had frustrated and bored her. But with us in the San Francisco History Room, this changed. When she asked for a file on Ocean Beach, the librarian told her there was none. She paused and then asked for Playland and Sutro Baths. She had figured out an alternative route to the information. As we turned over century-old photographs, she paused to assess different images, making judgments about contrast and detail, always thinking in terms of what would make a point for our film. Thumbing through the file on the Fillmore, Davinia suddenly held up an image. "This one is one we took. We stood in this same place." She was right.

No sooner did we have the photographs chosen than my students upped the ante. They decided to score the film with their own music. I taught social studies and language arts. I had stretched to photography, but I was musically illiterate. They wanted the music that the Advanced Band was working on, "In the Mood." They decided that it would "go great with the Sutro Baths." They wanted to fill those songs out with popular music, but after listening, decided they wanted their own beginner band pieces instead, even if it meant forming a new band from several different classes. Fine, but how could I direct work when I had no sense of what to look for, how to give feedback, or what was successful? When one of my students explained that the music teacher, Jack Martens, said he would lend us instruments and his practice room during our class time, I realized I did not have to go it alone. Jack runs a remarkable band program that is as much a class in responsibility and revising toward excellence as it is a class in rhythm and intonation. Sabrina, a student who had rarely stepped forward in my classes before this, shone with confidence as she assumed a leadership role, coordinating and directing students. She insisted on rehearsals where flawless performance was the rule. When a mistake occurred, students stopped, talked over the problem, and began again. Clearly, Jack had given them a common vocabulary for discussing the technical and artistic aspects of their music. And he had taught them that rehearsal and revision were the heart of good work—not an optional afterthought.

Jim's continuing work with students' photographs and historical images was an equally powerful source of revising and refining. The concrete examples of an image developed in different ways, or cropped to create an interesting composition, or a series of different frames of the same scene made the issues of choice tangible and interesting. We were not rich and we couldn't print every image. So students had to pore over their proof sheets. Jim wouldn't tell them what to print. They had to choose wisely (Figure 6–2).

FIGURE 6–2. *Proof Sheet with Chosen Image Circled*

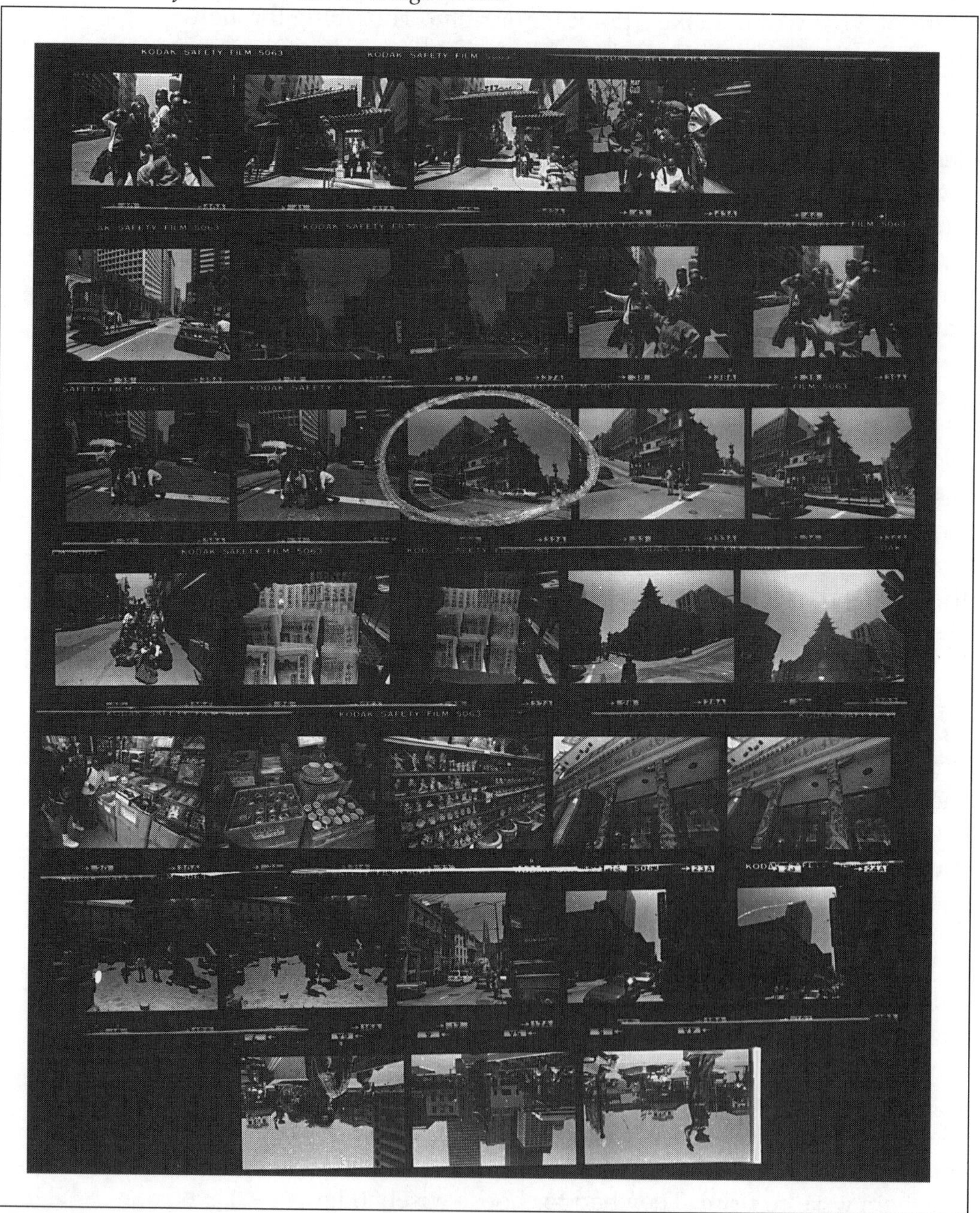

In this atmosphere, I knew that the film script deserved—and would get—the same attention. The final product would be a video made up of still photos, mostly taken by students, but interspersed with some historical photos we had chosen from the library. Students would narrate the film, and their original music would become the soundtrack. I hired a substitute for the day and set up an intense "Writers' Workshop" in another classroom. For each scene, I chose students who had emerged as the most interested in each place we visited. We pored over their journals and observational pieces to find writing that was as articulate as the images it was meant to accompany. We worked scene by scene, brainstorming ideas, which a recorder wrote down. We struggled toward the right order of ideas and images, with students resequencing photographs as their writing developed. As soon as the writing took form, a student would read it into the microphone and play it back for the group. Listening to themselves, students immediately recognized run-on sentences, lack of continuity, and repeated words. Revision was immediate. Possibly the small size of the groups made it easier to take criticism. The students' work was clearly informed by a defined task, a real audience, and a concrete deadline.

Meeting External Standards

The class worked in overdrive for the last three weeks of school. Jim threw a "World Premiere" party for the sixth grade. We invited the principal, Dianne Meltesen. All of us who had been there from the beginning were bowled over by the amount and quality of work. But would an outsider be able to see it? Would it seem like serious teaching and learning, or just some kind of extracurricular adventure?

The lights dimmed, the room grew still, and we were all glued to the video screen. The look on students' faces at the end of the twelve minutes of video was wordless proof of success. But I knew that Dianne would interview the students, probing deeper into what they had learned. She asked two simple questions: "What did you do?" and "How do you know you were successful?" In response to the first, students brainstormed this list:

We explored our neighborhoods through field trips.
We interviewed people.
We took photographs, developed and printed the pictures.
We read about different places and their histories.
We worked together.
We wrote.
We spoke.
We played music.
We learned about places and cultures.
We learned to do research and record our information.

How did they know they were successful?

We worked over a long period of time.
We completed a product.
We revised and reworked our project.
We worked well with others.
Our product looked good.
We got responses from audiences, adults, and peers.

These are many of the same goals we ask for in the schoolwide portfolios our eighth graders present as a part of graduating—but in the students' own words.

Reflections

If you look into the binders and folders of most middle-school students, you will find plenty of beginning "research projects" on mummies or pyramids, the state of California, or volcanoes. To conduct that research we offer students skills like how to do library searches, how to outline, and how to take notes; we give them the rules for writing bibliographies. But a project like "All Across San Francisco" suggests that we have overlooked an even more fundamental set of tools:

1. The invitation of the world outside the classroom. The churches in the Fillmore, the curling roofs in Chinatown, the stinging sand and sad, empty space at Ocean Beach commanded attention and urged questions. This kind of alertness and urgency are basic.

2. More languages than print. For many of my students the visual language of images was an absolutely necessary entry point. Many of them could use it immediately and intuitively. But at the same time, as Jim Crowley used it, it was another way to think about composition, messages, editing, and effects.
3. A sense for excellence. Both Jim Crowley and Jack Martens provided undeniable examples of what it was to craft and use visual or musical messages well. They were living examples of the refusal to compromise. They made revision contagious.
4. A genuine audience. My students knew we were making a video that would be shown to other students, the principal, and teachers. They worked toward that moment just as a band approaches a final concert.

Are these just gimmicks? Sugarcoating on the hard work of genuine research? I don't think so. To this day, I can be rushing down the hallway to make a phone call or get books for the next class, and a student from last year will stop me in the hall. He may want to borrow the film to show it to his uncle who is coming to visit. Or she may want to talk about whether this year's sixth graders are making a different film. Or to recall the trip through the Fillmore. Or Playland. They do so with a remarkable sense of authorship. They have been researchers and filmmakers. It is their responsibility to see that the craft is carried on. And they are right.

References

Coerr, Eleanor. 1994. *Sadako and the Thousand Paper Cranes.* New York: Dell.

Reflections from a Colleague

Cynthia Katz (Teacher, Concord, Massachusetts)

Reading Kamara Juarez's chapter, I found myself repeating "yes" and "of course" as I underlined and scribbled notes in the margins. I know photography—I live it and teach it. It can become one of the most immediate of the visual languages, once we teach students the necessary tools of craft and picture structure. That is, *if* our questions and proddings push them on. But visual as our culture has become, we often are starting almost from scratch. Exactly as Juarez points out, until we help students pursue and investigate to the point that they develop authorship, we will not see that richness of detail, personal vision, or critical insight. When we educate students in the making of photographs, training them to understand what makes strong work—the alliance of craft and vision, pursuit, being selective, reflecting, and then taking all that back and photographing more—we are training them to do good work in anything. Personal connection creates commitment. The grandmother who responded to the walking tour of the Fillmore by exclaiming, "What's there to see? There's nothing there," reminded me of why I work hard to show my students that nothing is too small to investigate. When you really look closely, using the frame of your camera as a personal way of selecting what you see, strong images result.

I was delighted to meet another teacher who realizes how learning photography and the resulting growth in visual literacy can connect to other disciplines. When Juarez spoke of the connection between making strong photographs and writing well, seeing both "as full of choice, style, collaboration, discussion, investigation, and editing," I felt another heart on my side. She saw her students learn a new vocabulary and "standards of thinking about their images as more than casual snapshots," and then put that to use both as makers of their own photographs and as critics and assessors of the work of others.

As a photographic educator, I was proud to see another teacher say out loud that her learners with problems found successes, and even became the leaders of the group once given the chance to make something that could have force and grace. In my own darkroom, I, like Kami, have seen "slow readers who found writing challenging" become critical readers of images. Each year I cultivate many of my own Sabrinas, "a student who had rarely stepped forward in my classes before this, shone with confidence as she assumed a leadership role . . ." Any teacher would remember the moment when Darnell asked a pivotal question for photographers: "Do we have to take it from here?" His changed vantage point resulted in his producing "a startling image." What Juarez did, with the help of her photographic and musical colleagues, was to create an interesting problem for her students, giving them tools so that they could become the owners of the information and the work. Photography is a great medium to allow kids to blow us away, because it is theirs. I see this all the time in my classes. When we as teachers push—asking key questions, imploring students to consider certain things, show connections, seek clarification—the deeper kids go and the richer and more complex the work becomes.

But the photography teacher in me wants to push further. I don't want my students to "take" photographs; I want them to "make" them. Making is more precise, more thoughtful, more extended. It allows them to go further. So I look at the Chinatown photograph, and a conversation with the young photographer runs through my head. I point out the linear aspects, the strong diagonals leading to an unknown point outside the image, and ponder what is outside the frame. I show the juxtaposition between the Western and Eastern architecture, and how the rectangular shapes of the trolley windows repeat and emphasize those in both the buildings. I muse aloud about the many directions she could go: emphasize the similarities, emphasize the differences, use other objects (people, cars, buses, trolleys, etc.) to create visual links or separations, questions.

Together, we glance at the contact sheet. I am looking for how the student pursues the subject, not just taking one picture here, one picture there, but finding something that interests her, and using her camera to investigate it. We talk about the images, vantage point, the moment, light. We talk about a visual narrative. I might suggest that she look at *Patterson* by George Tice, to see how another photographer documented a city—how the story of a place was told. Then she goes back and photographs again. I can see her caught up in the process of pursuing a vision, of finding a voice. A visual one. Going from *taking* to *making* pictures.

Epilogue

A Teacher's Manifesto

Julie Craven

In her introduction, Dennie Wolf mused about where to file this book. I don't want the book put away until we take up another question: Where does a thoughtful teacher file herself? I've lived in two of the worlds represented in these pages, that of the classroom teacher and that of the researcher/school reformer. The first compels with its vigorous reality while the second seduces with its professional sanity. Why, I want to know, can teachers so rarely have both worlds? I am angry at this either/or proposition. I want to stay in the classroom *and* feel professional. I want this not only for me, but also for the teacher-authors in this book, and for our countless other thoughtful colleagues. This book evokes a vision of a world in which we don't have to choose.

Reading these teachers' experiences, I reaffirm my love of the teacher's world. I share the thrill to the chase of that elusive goal: the melding of curriculum and classroom environment that helps young people be the best readers, writers, and thinkers they can be. I, too, seek that combination of hope and structure that can turn an ordinary descriptive paragraph into a sharp piece of journalism. In this world, I am a cheap date. When the girl who refuses to write unexpectedly asks to stay after to finish her essay; when a child pushes himself to finish his oral presentation even as tears stream down his face and then his classmates applaud his determination; when I see huddled together over a common problem the same heads that too often turn away from each other in the hallways—then the classroom is a beautiful place and teaching is clearly the profession for me.

But there are days when I would walk out of the world of teaching forever. How does a human, never mind a professional, eat lunch between 10:52 and 11:07 every day? Since when should the daily focus of my diagnostic powers be to deduce whether a child who asks to go to the bathroom is just looking for an excuse to leave the classroom? How do I find time to read articles on effective feedback when I look at homework from a hundred students each night? I am not alone in these frustrations. I can read between the lines of the teacher chapters in this book. I know the exhaustion of the search to find good journalism that students can read. I know the energy student placements and field trips demand: the calls from home because the classroom has no phone, the chase of the permission slips, and so on, and on. What teacher can endure this frantic chain of small imperatives—and think?

As teachers, we get occasional glimpses of the professional world outside of the classroom. Sometimes we sit on panels at portfolio conferences or participate in two-day workshops at National Council of Teachers of English conventions. But, frankly, these glimpses are all too brief. More rarely, our time in the professional world is extended. We take sabbaticals to work on a thesis, do research, or mentor others. Only then does the luxury of this world sink in. We have time to plan. We can read. We can have conversations with colleagues. We can revise and refine our plans. Being able to eat and go to the bathroom when we need to are icing on the cake.

The root of that luxury is, I think, opportunity for reflection. But how do we connect that reflection to improving classroom performance? For instance, when I stepped into the world of researcher/school reformer for a year, there was nowhere to try out my ideas. Without trial by fire, how could I really know if they worked? And if I didn't know that, how could I urge teachers to work in ways I only imagined? I lost touch with the reality I loved and needed in order to think seriously about what works in public education. For that, I realized I needed "my kids" back.

So I returned to the classroom with my dilemma still alive. But now I discuss it openly with colleagues. I am constantly asking how we can get hold of just those elements—time, thought, talk—

that would actually allow us to be professional teachers. This book and the curriculum seminars it grew out of suggest some answers. The curricula that these teachers developed for their students actually contain much that teachers yearn for. Each of these journalism projects nurtures a community of learners; each makes room for personal choice and real audiences. All the projects allow time for grappling with ideas, reflecting, and refining. None of this is by accident. All these teachers wanted "real world" creativity and sustained learning for their students.

With all the clarity of individuals who know what constraint, urgency, and routine can do to thought, we teachers need to rethink our own professional development so that we ask for ourselves all that is good for students. We need to claim ongoing intellectual life so that we can endure the chaos and routine. So here's my Teacher's Manifesto:

> We need curriculum projects that will allow us to work together on a shared task for several years, at minimum, not several days.

The teachers in this book have shown the value of creating a community of learners in their classrooms. They recognize that these communities need to be built over time, around real, shared projects like producing a video or a magazine. These communities clearly raise standards and build deeper collective understanding of "best work." In these communities students feel safe taking risks. They use each other as resources in peer reviews and group activities. In a world where students are no longer isolated in their learning, they thrive.

We teachers also thrive in a community of learners. Teaching is extremely isolating. The teachers who took part in the curriculum seminars worked together for nearly two years; we have all been part of PACE for five. When we spoke about the benefits of the seminars, there was a constant refrain: we relished being part of a collegial group working toward a common goal. We welcomed the critical feedback from peers and looked forward to gathering again to compare progress and seek more feedback. Collectively, we have pushed the standards for demanding curriculum higher than what existed in our individual classrooms. School boards and departments of education should foster more such communities. Don't require twenty disconnected hours of "professional development" for recertification; instead, bring together language arts teachers three times a year for two years, and charge them with developing units on immersion journalism, or poetry, or whatever aspect of the writing curriculum they want to invigorate.

> We need to work in ways that allow both a common focus on key elements and enough flexibility so that we can adapt those core ideas to the particular characteristics of our classrooms.

The student work in this book shows students using their learning experiences to make sense of their worlds. Their teachers have set common standards, but because they value the uniqueness of each child's experiences, they have also built elements of choice into what students learn and how they present it. Professional-development structures need that same combination of commonality and flexibility. Contrary to the premise implied by the many workshops that present interesting units as packaged pieces, curriculum is not transportable. It is not a mix to which one adds water and stirs. Rather, it is a recipe that we adapt, like all practical cooks, to our particular tastes and needs. What we need is explicit support in how to do this well. In other words, we want culinary experience with a chef that inspires us to create our own daring new concoctions. Witness the results of the curriculum seminars. Hand in hand with a "real world expert," teachers undertook a common project, operated within a common schedule with common checkpoints, yet still had the autonomy to produce a range of products that includes a video and a magazine. We can all produce meaningful curriculum this way. When the language-arts teachers come together for two years to develop poetry units, they should first meet in the fall to agree upon common poetry standards. Then they should expect each other to design and implement a unit by spring, meeting once more for ideas and support before actually implementing their units. At the end of the first year, they should reflect jointly upon how well each unit met the common and particular learning goals, then revise and reteach their units in the second year.

If teachers are to have greater autonomy in curriculum projects, we need to avoid another potential pitfall of traditional workshops, where too often pieces are taken from the whole and implemented, but the essential elements that made the unit a powerful episode in learning are lost. In this scenario, teachers return to their classes to present an interesting activity without ever questioning their classroom practice. We need to sustain professional development in the real sense—through structures and experiences that help us identify assumptions we have about teaching and learning, challenge us to reflect on their validity, and support us to make real changes that reflect our newfound understanding of what is important and what is pedagogically sound. Hence the final points of my manifesto:

> Curriculum projects need to be experientially based so that teachers can grapple with ideas and skills they want to teach.

All the teachers in this book refer to their experiences as immersion journalists as they plan the learning experiences for their students. They recall the fear, the excitement, and the pride, and they use those recollections to inform their planning. If we want to make classrooms engaging, meaningful places for students, we need to be engaged; we must have found meaning for ourselves. When we build units on poetry, mentor us in being poets; when we design research projects, guide us in conducting our own surveys, compiling our own data, and drawing and supporting our own conclusions.

> We need to examine student work and keep that examination at the center of every stage of our joint work.

The goal of developing strong curriculum is to improve student learning, not to create beautifully presented lessons. We need to keep track of that goal. Like teaching, the units portrayed in this book are not polished pieces, they are works in progress. When we design curriculum, we should do as the teachers in the curriculum seminars. We should start with a student in mind whom we want to reach more effectively. We should include examples of that student's work when we present drafts of our units. We should give and receive feedback on how well a unit and our teaching address that student's needs. At the end of the year, when we gather again to evaluate the effectiveness of our curricula, we should bring with us artifacts of student learning throughout the course of the unit: videos of conversations; student journals; final projects that include the different stages of the creative process, like brainstorms, drafts, and peer reviews. We should examine these artifacts for evidence of learning and use what we see to make decisions for the next unit and next year. The cycle should continue.

> Teachers need publication opportunities for presenting and reflecting on the results of our projects.

The "ah-ha's" that light up a teacher's world happen as students struggle to make enough sense of what they are learning so that they can present it successfully to an audience outside of their classroom. Teachers grow this way, too. In my year at PACE, I wrote up units I had taught into models for our seminars. In the process, what for me had been instinctive suddenly became explicit. Ah-ha. I gained insight into my teaching that gave me an energizing confidence and focus when I returned to the classroom.

I observe similar "ah-ha's" in the chapters of this book. I worked with all these people from the beginning of the seminars to the publication of this book. I know the agony we all went through to produce the final manuscript. In the process, we came away with a clearer idea of how to support teachers. More significantly for professional development, these teachers returned to their own classrooms with a deeper understanding of what they want to provide for their students, why they want to provide it, and how to do so most successfully. We want more of this experience. Teachers should have more opportunities to write about their work—even publish books. Districts should give us a release day once a month, and expect us to publish an article once a year. Let us choose our audiences—a magazine, the local paper, a parent newsletter—and we will find something we want to say.

So that's my Teacher's Manifesto. I want for teachers the structures and experiences that the teachers in this book want for their students. In that way, teachers can be in the classroom *and* be professional. We shouldn't have to choose.

Contributors

Lee Gutkind is founder and editor of the journal *Creative Nonfiction*. Former director of the writing program at the University of Pittsburgh and currently professor of English, Mr. Gutkind is the author of several books and essays, including his award-winning *Many Sleepless Nights* and *Stuck in Time, The Tragedy of Childhood Mental Illness*.

Carol Kuhl Barry teaches sixth grade English/language arts and science at Muirlands Middle School in the San Diego Unified School District. She has served as a teacher-participant and consultant in both the Writing to Learn and PACE projects. Ms. Barry has presented at several National Middle School Association meetings, and was a recipient of a Council for Basic Education's National Fellowship for Independent Study.

Kellie Brown is a teacher at William James Middle School in Fort Worth, Texas, where she teaches sixth and seventh grade English and social studies. Currently, she is involved in the Applied Learning program in her district as well as the New Standards Project and Harvard PACE.

Kamara Juarez teaches sixth grade social studies and language arts at Benjamin Franklin Middle School in San Francisco. Ms. Juarez is very enthusiastic about life and tries to instill this energy into her students. She is interested in creating projects that reach across the disciplines.

Linda Reilly has taught in the Rochester City School District for thirteen years, most recently as an ESOL teacher. Currently, she teaches at Thomas Jefferson Middle School in L.E.A.P. (Learning through English Academic Program), a sheltered English program for immigrants who are new arrivals in the United States.

Connie Russell-Rodriguez teaches middle-school humanities at the Rafael Hernandez School in Boston. The Hernandez is one of the original schools involved in Expeditionary Learning/Outward Bound, a design of the New American Schools Design Corporation.

Kelly Peacock Wright teaches English to seventh grade students at Muirlands Middle School in the San Diego Unified School District. Ms. Peacock Wright's professional experiences include involvement in Harvard PACE, the New Standards Project, and California's CLAS/ETS portfolio pilot.